Additive Free

TIPPING SACRED COWS

The Uplifting Story of Spilt Milk and Finding Your Own Spiritual Path in a Hectic World

BETSY CHASSE

ATRIA PAPERBACK
New York London Toronto Sydney New Delhi

BEYOND WORDS
Hillsboro, Oregon

ATRIA PAPERBACK
A Division of Simon & Schuster, Inc.
1230 Avenue of the Americas
New York, NY 10020

BEYOND WORDS
20827 N.W. Cornell Road, Suite 500
Hillsboro, Oregon 97124-9808
503-531-8700 / 503-531-8773 fax
www.beyondword.com

Managing editor: Lindsay S. Brown
Editors: Anna Noak, Sarah Heilman
Copyeditor: Meadowlark Publishing Services
Proofreader: Michelle Blair
Interior Design: Devon Smith
Composition: William H. Brunson Typography Services

First Atria Paperback/Beyond Words trade paperback edition January 2014

ATRIA PAPERBACK and colophon are trademarks of Simon & Schuster, Inc.
Beyond Words Publishing is an imprint of Simon & Schuster, Inc. and the Beyond Words logo is a registered trademark of Beyond Words Publishing, Inc.

For more information about special discounts for bulk purchases, please contact Simon & Schuster Special Sales at 1-866-506-1949 or business@simonandschuster.com.

The Simon & Schuster Speakers Bureau can bring authors to your live event. For more information or to book an event, contact the Simon & Schuster Speakers Bureau at 1-866-248-3049 or visit our website at www.simonspeakers.com.

Manufactured in the United States of America

10 9 8 7 6 5 4 3 2 1

Library of Congress Cataloging-in-Publication Data

Chasse, Betsy.
    Tipping sacred cows : the uplifting story of spilt milk and finding your own spiritual path in a hectic world / Betsy Chasse.
        pages   cm
    Includes bibliographical references.
    1. Philosophy—Miscellanea. 2. Ideology—Miscellanea. 3. Spiritual life. I. Title.
BF1999.C517 2014
204—dc23

                                                                                    2013028468

ISBN 978-1-58270-460-9
ISBN 978-1-4767-4472-8 (ebook)

The corporate mission of Beyond Words Publishing, Inc.: *Inspire to Integrity*

Contents

What do sad people have in common?
It seems they have all built a shrine to the past
and often go there and do a strange wail and worship.
What is the beginning of happiness?
It is to stop being so religious
like that.

—*The Gift: Poems by Hafiz, The Great Sufi Master*,
translated by Daniel Ladinsky

Foreword

I first met Betsy Chasse at a dinner party. As we caught a glance of each other that night, she immediately approached me with a strikingly bold and confident demeanor. The next thing I knew, we were engaged in a very robust and direct conversation about life. I was struck by the type of unique questions she asked me. The energy of our exchange and the velocity of our dialogue took us deep into a volley about the nature of reality. In a matter of moments, I found that we shared something in common. We are both pragmatists.

One of the founding fathers of pragmatism is a hero of mine, the great author, physician, and psychologist William James. James created a doctrine in which the meaning of an idea, a concept, or a proposition lies in its observable practical consequences. In other words, when you learn something new, how are you going to "practically" apply that philosophical information to create a favorable experience in your life?

Well, that's kind of how our conversation unfolded that night.

We discussed the latest research about the brain and body, the mind, and consciousness as well as the exciting theoretical discoveries in quantum physics. Betsy cross-examined me about the quantum model of reality. I remember her asking, "Do you believe that your subjective mind has an effect on the objective world?"

I knew I was in for a long night.

We talked about the most up-to-date research in brain imaging, neuroplasticity, epigenetics, and psychoneuroimmunology. It was a great conversation. We agreed that all of these new sciences are suggesting expanded possibilities on how to move toward implementing what we innately know about our real potential. I told her that science has become the contemporary language of spirituality. And when we combine all of the new understandings in science, we can begin to demystify the mystical.

This is by far one of my passions—I have a sincere interest in demystifying the mystical so that every person understands that we have, within our reach, all we need to make significant changes in our lives. The truth be told, we come preloaded with all of the neurological and biological machinery to make this possible.

But how do we personalize these philosophical idealisms when we are a single parent with three children, struggling financially, and are suffering from a chronic pain disorder? This book will give you real guidance into knowing how to demonstrate these concepts by seeing the process through the eyes of someone like Betsy. She gives you real life experiences to relate to and certainly dispels the much-needed dogmas of spirituality. Someone has to do it and I can't think of a better person.

I believe that this is a time in history when not only do people want to "know," they want to "know how." *How* do we apply both emerging scientific concepts and age-old wisdom to succeed at living a more enriched life? When you and I can connect the dots of what science is discovering about the nature of reality, and when we give ourselves permission to apply those principles to the simplest measures in our day-to-day existence, we then become both a mystic and a scientist in our own reality.

But we should never wait for science to give us permission to do the uncommon; if we do, then we are turning science into another religion. We should be brave enough to contemplate our lives, do what we feared was "outside the box," and do it repeatedly. When we do that, we are on our way to a greater level of personal empowerment.

We are in the age of information because of advancements in technology. But all of this information that is available to us is to *do* something with—otherwise it's just good dinner conversation, isn't it? Betsy Chasse is not a dinner conversationalist and neither am I.

If all of us can open our minds to the way things really are, and let go of our conditioned beliefs about life and ourselves, shouldn't we see the fruits of our efforts? In the process of that discovery, however, we might have to tip a few sacred cows along the way. This book is about changing your mindset and embracing what's real and what's not.

If you take intellectual information that you learn as a *philosophy*, and then *initiate* that knowledge into your life by applying it enough times until you *master* it, you will ultimately move from being a philosopher to an initiate to a master. There is sound scientific evidence that this is possible; however, you will most certainly be challenged along the way.

In the pages that follow, you will learn that personal transformation is a process. It is a daily step-by-step, conscious effort. To break free from the hardwired programs, social conditioning, and emotional memories that keep us anchored to the past will require that you stop yourself from going unconscious. That's how true change happens. Nevertheless, we should never lie to ourselves and think it's a linear process. We have to be realistic about the journey and never excuse ourselves with self-imposed beliefs about spirituality.

When you look into the mirror, you see your reflection, and you know who you are seeing is the physical you. But how does the true self, the ego and the soul, see itself? Your life is a mirror image of your mind, your consciousness, and who you really are. There are no schools of ancient spiritual wisdom sitting high on mountaintops in the Himalayas waiting to initiate us into becoming mystics and saints. Our life is our initiation into greatness. You and I should see life as an opportunity to reach greater and greater levels of self so that we can overcome our own limitations with more expanded levels of mind. That's how the pragmatist, instead of the victim, sees it.

To abandon the familiar ways that we think about life, and have grown accustomed to in order to embrace new paradigms, will feel so unnatural. Frankly, it takes effort—and it's uncomfortable. Why? Because we will no longer feel like ourselves.

How many times in history have admirable individuals who struggled against outdated beliefs been considered heretics and fools, yet after having endured the abuse of average minds emerged as geniuses, saints, or masters? In time, they became supernatural.

But how do we become supernatural? We have to begin to do what is unnatural: It is *to give* in the midst of crisis when everyone is feeling lack and poverty; *to love* when everyone is angry and judging others; *to demonstrate* courage and peace when everyone else is in fear; *to show kindness* when there is hostility and aggression; *to surrender to possibility* when the rest of the world is aggressively pushing to be first and competing on the way to the endless top; and *to knowingly smile* in the face of adversity. It seems so unnatural to make these types of choices in the midst of such experiences, but if we repeatedly succeed, in time we will transcend the norm.

So I invite you to experiment with everything that you learn in this book, and to objectively observe the outcomes. If you make the effort to change your inner world of thoughts and feelings, your external environment should begin to give you feedback to show you that your mind has had an effect on your "outer" world. Why else would you do it?

As an educator in the fields of neuroscience, brain function, biology, and brain chemistry, I have been privileged to be at the forefront of some of this research—not just by studying these fields but also by observing the effects of this new science once applied by common people like you and me. That's the moment when the possibilities of this new science become reality.

Betsy Chasse's work is an invitation to "practice life" with honest spirituality. I hope you enjoy this book as much as I did.

Dr. Joe Dispenza, author of *You Are the Placebo,*
Breaking the Habit of Being Yourself, and *Evolve Your Brain*

Preface

How to Get Coldcocked by an Epiphany
(or Waking Up Can Suck or Not Suck Depending on How You Handle Your Shit)

Think left and think right and think low and think high. Oh, the thinks you can think up if only you try!
—Dr. Seuss, *Oh The Things You Can Think!*

There was a time when my life was easy, or so I thought. I was happily living in my shoe-consciousness—where I was all about the shoes I was wearing, the car I was driving, and the boyfriend I was dating (and his car and his shoes)—and avoiding like the plague any existential quest that might lead me into the deep, dark bowels of my soul. Such a quest would involve passing through some shit and, well, hanging out in my soul-bowels seemed less than appealing.

And I suppose that's the story of most twentysomethings, but as my thirties approached, the clock started ticking, and the search for the meaning of anything and everything kicked into gear. Miraculously, I was handed the golden egg, the holy grail of spiritual understanding on a silver platter, or rather on the silver screen, in the form of *What the Bleep Do We Know!?*, the movie I co-created with Will Arntz and Mark Vicente. Chock-full of spiritual know-how gathered from magical movie making, I knew it all *and* owned some great shoes. Enlightenment? Check!

I quickly followed up on my spiritual mastery and manifested the perfect husband, beautiful children, and a gorgeous home. Finally, everything clicked. My inner and outer selves were accessorized, matched, and decked out in deep-ish thoughts and somewhat-understandings. It was a perfect balance of beliefs that allowed me to coast along, riding high on my newfound enlightenment.

So there I was. I had my "spirituality" all laid out for me, picked up from the latest and greatest minds I'd conned my way into meeting. My beliefs lazed like cows standing in a pasture of protection, all blinged out, while I worked really hard to keep them all sparkly, running from cow to cow in my awesome new boots.

And let me tell you, I frolicked the hell out of that pasture, leaping through the air, twirling, and all the other stuff you do when you frolic. I frolicked right up until I slipped on something smelly and fell, and really, what was I expecting? I was in a freaking cow pasture, for God's sake.

Splat, squish, my boots! I actually heard cartoon sounds when I landed. Okay, I didn't, but I should have, it was that kind of absurd. I lay there, all sprawled out, seeing my pasture and my cows from a hoof-level perspective. I saw the ground on which was built my understanding of the world and who I was in my little part of time and space. In that moment, I came to one profound realization: my pasture of perfection was full of shit, and it reeked. It was a wake-you-up kind of smell. My life imploded, and it stank. Cue life-altering epiphany, ready or not (most likely *not*, because who's really ready to completely throw out everything you thought you knew and start from scratch?).

I'd heard about such things—great epiphanies that illuminate some kind of knowledge and understanding into a higher state of being, an evolution of the spirit and/or mind. My friends would often sit around the fire, spinning their tales about how, after fasting or meditating or pilgrimaging or a combo of the three (or helping at a homeless shelter or doing work with the sick or some other selfless activity or maybe even seeing someone else perform an act of kindness, shit, even reading about it in the paper), a person felt compelled to evaluate their life. Then, in the story, the person comes to some kind of spiritual jackpot and goes about the business of saving the world, or at least a section of it, while brimming with joy and spreading compassion like creamy peanut butter on a perfect PB&J.

My cow pie epiphany was so far removed from the miraculous one of landing smack-dab in the middle of a New Age phenomenon of quantum mysticism, complete with a walk on the red carpet, princess dress, and handsome prince (I mean, how does a girl who has never even spelled the words *quantum physics* end up making a movie about how it's the end all, be all of the meaning of life?) that the mind boggles. When you soar that high, your epiphany is bound to be messy.

Probably because I was no June Cleaver and never mastered the art of the perfect PB&J; mine always have jelly dripping out the bottom, staining my kids' shirts and making their hands all sticky, with my own shirt being quickly used as a napkin by my little problem solvers, because of course I forgot to give them one of those. In my life, I never seemed to have a napkin when I needed one, even though looking at me, you would probably think to yourself, *how does she do it?*

I was an excellent faker.

I produced illusionary napkins at will, all smoke and mirrors. People will see what they want to see, especially if the magician is really good, and I was. Unfortunately, my superpower of producing an endless supply of immaterial napkins was less than awesome. At this moment, with this epiphany, catastrophic as it was going to be when the full implications spilled out into my life, I needed the real deal because it would take every napkin on the planet to clean up the mess.

My awesome epiphany was like this: imagine yourself waking up next to your sleeping husband and feeling this overwhelming urge to scream BURGLAR! Only, I was the burglar in this scenario, and I had stolen someone's entire life—the house, the bed, the husband—*everything*. Then, ironically, I realized that I had stolen fake goods.

My epiphany came on like hives—a slow burn of discomfort between the carpool and cleaning up cat vomit. It culminated one morning when all of my beliefs, my understanding of my carefully built system of daily agreements about the way life is, tipped and fell domino-like, leaving me with the task of trying to stand them all up again.

I did not know how I ended up in that situation that morning, not then. It just happened like life does. Whammo—mornings and existential angst, slipping into my bedroom window, poking at me.

I did not receive this wake-up call well; I am not a morning person. I need time before I move, time to lie there and bemoan the fact that I have to do things, like open my eyes and clean the litter box.

On that morning, I lay in the wandering-void-of-not-willing-to-be-awake, that gray space between silent room and loud thoughts, and found the first cow to which the title of this book refers, and it was definitely tipped. The cow called *I am*. I know this because in that in-between moment, I realized I wasn't who I thought I was. I was a fraud, an alien. Illegal, a stranger in a strange land, with a husband lying next to me and kids down the hall.

I watched the pieces of my life come together like a mosaic above me, little shards of colored glass, each representing a belief I held sacred, an idea about what was real and what was true about myself and everything I thought made sense, everything I thought about what it meant to live a spiritual life. I watched my understanding of what the word spiritual meant, what anything meant, the minutia of the moments that brought me here, to this suddenly unfamiliar life, and I was filled with an unwelcome sense of hurt and sadness.

I felt as if I had been abandoned by my cows, left to survive in this house filled with children, a spouse, a dog, and a couple of cats. All of them felt alien to me. How was it possible, with all I had in my life, that I could feel so profoundly unhappy and unfulfilled? And it went beyond a feeling. I became it in every fiber of myself—my skin and hair, my muscle and bone—they all became this unbearable feeling until it felt as if it was in my cells, changing me, making me heavy in a way I had never thought I could be. And worse, I did not understand it; I did not know how I had gotten to this moment. I had no sense of where it would go. I had no sense of any other way to be. All of this washed over me, the weight of it. How much my heart hurt took my breath away.

We've all had those moments in our lives when we feel stripped naked and empty, when a sudden realization about our life has pulverized us. Not knowing what else to do that morning, I first checked in on the usual suspect when we women sink into a pit of utter despair: could it be PMS? Bleeding for several days without dying can cause anyone to want to check out to another dimension. Nope, no such luck. Perhaps a cup of coffee and a smoke would snap me out of my soul-destroying moodiness. There is nothing like a morning visit from Juan Valdez and the Marlboro Man to bring a girl back from the brink.

I envisioned these boys gallantly bursting into my room and whisking me off to better pastures, a place where coffee and cigarettes solved all of life's problems. In my daydream, we sat together, discussing the big questions like *Why am I here?* and *Why am I living this life?* with some *Is this it?* added in. Talking Heads' "Once in a Lifetime" played in the background, and my trusty copy of Ekhart Tolle's *The Power of Now* sat close by for easy reference.

I played out that scenario in my head and realized that my boys Juan and the Marlboro Man did not have the answers I sought, and neither did I. I froze, because I had never before been without an answer. My sacred cows had always been able to muster a fresh-milked glass of magic—instant pasteurized 2-percent to quench my existential thirst. In retrospect (and to really push this metaphor home), I realize I had been drinking powdered milk that was not quite mixed in all the way, still grainy and like sandpaper in my mouth. I always just thought that was the way it was supposed to be.

Instead of answers, my Juan and the Man fantasy gave me a WTF enema: you know, that hollow empty feeling you get when your shit has been sucked out and it's sitting next to you in a bag, and you can actually see all the crap you've stuffed into yourself. There they were, all the moments in my life leading up to this one, all the platitudes and pithy one-liners meant to ease a person into that false sense of thinking they know when really they don't, in a bag smelling strongly of self-delusion.

Crazily enough, the thought of drinking liquid black asphalt and puffing on a nicotine bomb suddenly didn't seem so appealing on this particular morning.

I've never been good at depriving myself, especially when it comes to caffeine and nicotine. Those have always been my usual go-to problem solvers—I mean, if Eckhart and Deepak couldn't help, usually a smoke and a mocha could, and without them, I was cranky and pissed off and suffered a robust bout of self-accountability dehydration. It seems to be a thing that when adults feel deprived, we generally either feel victimized or bitter. Out of the two, I'm better at bitter, which means blaming everyone I know.

The morning of The Epiphany (yes, it is now capitalized because it was an Event), I hopped right to it and blamed my parents, my husband, my kids, and even the damn cats—fur balls, always tortured, never happy with anything, always "me me me." They were all sucking the life out of me because they all obviously hated me and wanted to stifle me. The horrific conspiracy to keep me down was real, and the cats were in on it. Of course, the whole it-is-everyone's-fault-but-mine argument didn't hold water for long. It takes a lot of energy to blame the world, and there I was without even the help of a cup of coffee or a cigarette.

This is how it is when you have a crisis of self in the early morning, before the first nervanic drink of coffee, before the first puff of nicotine, before those things that pull you right back into shoe-consciousness. This is how it is, so you doubt the realness of everything. Nothing feels true.

And when nothing feels true, every bit of you freezes in place. You feel the inner you tremble. You feel it in your intellect and your heart, and most pointedly in your spirit. And you are filled with a horrible sense that you have caused yourself true harm. That's what it was for me, that moment in my bed, with my spirit trembling in actual, real fear.

As I lay in my bed, suspended in time, not able to move forward and unwilling to go back to pre-Epiphany ignorance (because once the shit's out, there's no putting it back), I realized the truth was I didn't know anything. Anything about happiness, love, spirituality, or myself . . . nothing, nada, zilch. Now that's a real what-the-fuck moment.

I will say, I was righteously indignant. My inner monologue was all: How is this even possible? I am an expert, dammit. I made a movie about creating reality and finding spiritual bliss, for the love of God! I've spent years reading the books, listening to the gurus, the speakers—I've collected some kick-ass wisdom. Look at my beautiful, gorgeous, painted cows, decorated and accessorized with everything I have learned.

Meanwhile, from a very cinematic-esque distance, I heard another voice challenging my convictions. The voice was very practical and even-toned—the voice of someone telling it like it is and speaking the truth. It said, "Betsy, if you are real with yourself, you will admit that you have no idea what happiness and bliss look like or what something like spirituality even means. Your herd of sacred cows, no matter how you fancy them up, are hanging out in a closed-off pasture full of crap. They are glass cows. Easily breakable glass cows, and it only took one small, real moment to break them. It's time to really wake the fuck up to reality—Love you!" I paraphrase, but that was the gist.

"So now what are we going to do?" my freaked-out, inner monologue squeaked. And I said, "Fuck if I know!"

What the bleep *did* I know?

Up until this moment, I had believed the story I was living; I had based myself, my identity, on being the expert, the mom, the wife, and the cat and dog owner. I had based myself on a story I told myself. I built my life around a belief that I had to be perfect, that no one could ever know the doubt and pain I felt inside me. My career was built upon being in the know—if anyone saw that I didn't know, I would be left with nothing, sort of like how I felt at that very moment. I had told myself that I should be happy at all costs, that I was seeking enlightenment, that screaming positive affirmations at the top of my lungs would eventually drown out the negative ones I whispered. I told myself that eventually that thing called the Law of Attraction would kick in, that I could indeed manifest all the gold I could imagine if only I meditated long enough, even if I never actually believed I deserved it. That didn't matter. Just be it, and it will be—right?

I would fake it until I made it.

It was all a lie; I was the fool, fooling me. At that moment I could not identify the person at the core of all of those labels. My story was myth, something to give me cognitive comfort in the dark night of my soul, or rather, in my case, in the cold light of day.

I have to say, even in retrospect I have no idea how long this little life disemboweling took. I did at some point realize that I needed to start fresh, from the ground up.

Yeah, that's easy to say, but after you've read all the perky platitudes on Facebook, how do you actually create a new life when you don't know *who* you're creating it for? And how do you create this "new" life if you don't know how you created the life you're already living?

Still lying in my bed, staring up at the ceiling, I started playing through, like a montage cliché, the movie of my life: every piece, every story, every truth, every belief from my faith to my lack thereof, everything I thought I knew. And one by one I dismantled all of it, leaving no room to justify my story, to placate it, or to appease it with the logic and illusion my sacred cows had previously so easily provided for me. One by one I ticked the pieces off: marriage—lie; wealth—lie; spiritual know-it-all—big, fat lie.

I checked them off until I could no longer hide behind the false reality I knew I had tried my hardest to make real. I confirmed that none of it was real, none of it was true, and that I was, in fact, an imposter in my own life. It was somewhat nauseating, this self-evisceration.

The mosaic of images that swirl before you during this self-examination, the moments from your past that flash before your eyes when you are peeling yourself back, are not the ones you want to remember. They're not the birthdays that made you laugh until you cried and the first kisses that made you touch your lips with your fingertips after they were done. No, instead they are the moments like when you lied to your best friend about kissing her boyfriend and when you first realized you could only fly in your dreams. You see the moment when your favorite stuffed animal remains silent instead of speaking to you when you cry into it at night. You see the moments filling you up with your life's heartbreak.

You see the things that made you lose your belief in magic and wild possibility and the things that made you exchange wonder and awe for fear of failure and the loss of your own love of self.

I saw all of this, all right there in front of me, in wonderful Technicolor on my ceiling. Plus a single statement in easy-to-understand words, flashing bright and glittery: YOU DID THIS TO YOURSELF.

That was a truth I wasn't sure I wanted to face. And let's be honest—who would? I was scared shitless.

In my Technicolor autobiography on the ceiling, I found that I had chosen the easiest path in my life. It wasn't a path that was filled with truth, and deep inside, I knew it. I had taken the story that was offered by the world at large, the one that took the least effort on my part, and ran with it, even when it hurt.

I have to say, I was an excellent runner. I even had a baton to pass along—my story of least resistance and even less internal work—and somewhere along the way, I decided I should collect lots of even less-stellar batons. Here, quick, take it: "You're too damaged to be worth anything to anyone." Here, quick, take it: "You're short and will never be pretty." Here, quick, take it: "You aren't smart enough for college, and you don't have the money." Here, quick, take it: "Just think happy thoughts and everything will be okay." Quick, run: "Make a movie about quantum physics and finally you will have the answers you seek."

All the while, I was grabbing a baton and running, grabbing and running, grabbing and running, until I couldn't hold any more batons and my legs burned and my feet had blisters and I couldn't breathe. I was desperate to grab on to that one baton that would deliver me to some kind of bliss, to enlightenment, to ubiquitous, amorphous happiness.

And while I was grabbing all of those batons, I was also busy passing out the ones I had constructed out of all the rest. All of my friends, my family, my kids, my dog, and even the damn cats, they took those DIY batons because that was all I handed them.

As I lay there buried under the batons I had grabbed, I began to realize that this life wasn't creating itself. There was an artist, a painter, a hand of God, if you will, up there somewhere, putting the pieces together. I saw my own hand reaching toward my pieces of glass, and I understood. There was a bit of wisdom to be found among my cows: it was up to me to create myself.

The clichés are true. With every yin there is a yang, with every down an up, and the upside to this ah-ha! moment—this Epiphany—was that I had a choice whether to believe the story or create a new one.

So often, we glom onto that new thing, that new book, that new technique, only to have our shelves become so cluttered with pretty glass cows that we lose sight of the blueprints, the unadorned cows underneath. We lose the ability to see their true beauty, their true meaning, and most important, their meaning to us. It was time to drop some batons. It was time to tip some sacred cows and chip off the bling.

I started with my own beliefs about myself, about what I thought I knew about what it meant to live a meaningful, spiritual life. It was time to figure out what being spiritual even meant, what any of it meant, and how I could finally find peace with it within myself.

I may have spent as many years on this journey as you have, or perhaps fewer. I had a lot of data, yet I hadn't really done the work to actually incorporate my knowledge about the stuff that fills us up and gives meaning to our lives, all of the things that I had researched and explored. I started to, but then got caught up in the pageantry, the illusion that a little bit of knowledge can cause you to build, and I left those cows on my shelf of intellectual pursuit. Yet I truly thought I had integrated everything. I guess that is part of the journey. I had peeled away layers of the onion of how we find meaning. But the work and application—that's the trick, isn't it?

Back in the day, in the early stages of my "awakening" when I first began to dig, little bits of myself were being revealed that I didn't like. Instead of digging further, I stopped because I was truly afraid of what I might find down there and afraid of what others might think of me if I wasn't perfect, if I didn't already know it all.

The morning of The Epiphany was the beginning of the next part of my journey. It began as I picked up one sacred cow of my past and really examined it from every angle, not just what was on top, but in those dips and curves that are usually hidden and always filled with hard-to-shake-up dust. I couldn't start the journey forward until I had cleaned up the mess I'd left behind, at least for myself. There is no going back and undoing, and I realized I didn't want to. I just wanted the freedom to leave it behind if I needed to, or take it with me, cleaned up and ready for use. It didn't have to be perfect, just workable. When you decide to hit the reset button in life, you can't always just hop on a plane and disappear off into the sunset. There is a reality you have created, and for me it was filled with a husband, children, cats, a dog, a career, a house, and shoes.

The greatest gift I have been given during this process is the freedom to break free of the old paradigm, the old patterns of myself, and to gleefully romp through my fields of cows and tip them at will. I know that when I do, I am experiencing a whole new reality (the one where I keep the kids, the cats, and the dog, but not the husband).

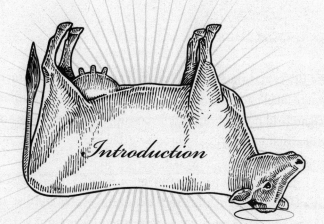

Introduction

Spirituality Is Just a Word, until It's Not,
and Other Revelations (or Tipping Sacred Cows)

What is a sacred cow? It is defined as an idea, custom, or institution considered to be exempt from criticism or questioning. Our world has a lot of sacred cows. In the United States, our biggie is the Constitution. No one had better mess with that foudning document. It is the glue that holds our pieces together. That document is treated as sacrosanct, as if the words printed there are directly from God. Speaking of God, we don't want to mess with that sacred cow either, especially the one found in those other famous sets of prose—the Tanakh, the Bible, and the Koran. Question any of these documents and you're liable to be labeled either unpatriotic, a heathen, or a pagan, and no one wants to be considered one of those ungodly, idol-worshiping, ritual-blood-sacrificing, self-indulgent social nihilists!

I realized my calling as an ungodly, idol-worshipping, ritual-blood-sacrificing, self-indulgent social nihilist or, as I like to call me, a spiritual seeker, when I was eight years old on a Sunday outing with my father, a choir director at multiple churches in our community. I had spent a not-delightful couple of hours of shaking in my fancy dress shoes after hearing that I was probably going to rot eternally in hell for secretly wishing my sister would run away so I could have her bedroom. I mean, I didn't really want my sister to run away; I just wanted her room and that seemed like the only way I was going to get it. I was confused by the contradiction of an all-loving God who would banish an eight-year-old to eternal damnation just over thinking about wanting her sister's bedroom. Was coveting my sister's room in my daydreams really that serious? Apparently, yes.

I spent the day watching and judging any possible negative thought that might cross me off God's waiting list into heaven for good girls, waiting for the skies to open and a big burly guy with a beard to glower down at me and, with a flick of his finger, zap me instantly into hell.*

My father, the man I believed knew everything, the one person in my life who would surely save me from eternal damnation, the man with the answers, could not explain this to me. And if he couldn't, then it was complete madness and I should steer clear of anything spiritual, lest I get lost forever in the burning fires of hell. Those people take their cows very seriously, and I wasn't about to mess with them. So from that moment on, I left the spiritual world behind and planted my fancy dress-up shoes firmly in material reality—safe, where what you see is what you get, where you could touch it, smell it, and taste it—and I liked it that way.

It isn't just forms of government and organized religions that have sacred cows. They're everywhere: in sports, in art, in movies, in pop culture, and in books. Most people take their sports cows very seriously. The same goes for their art cows, political cows, ethical and moral cows, and any and all of the cultural cows you can think of. But most especially, people take seriously the cows they hold on to about themselves and their individual beliefs.

One of the biggest sacred cows I have come across is the idea of what is spiritual. What does it mean to live a spiritual life? In my line of work, I spend a lot of time meeting people and talking with them about spirituality and all the sacred cows that go along with it. These cows include everything from making the quantum idea be the answer to all our questions to living the Law of Attraction, from whether emotions are bad or good or to be judged at all to whether to kill the ego or let it live. They even include the definition of enlightenment. I would often spend hours in conversations with people where I felt like we were all speaking different languages because everybody had their own ideas about what these things meant. No one wanted to give up their personal definition for a more global one we could all circle around, lest they be deemed less spiritual by the people they had deemed to be the mostest in the spiritual category. It was their sacred cow.

I once asked someone what she actually meant when she used words like *spirituality* and *bliss*. She gave me kind of a dumbfounded look and asked or, more like, exclaimed, "You don't know?!" And then she happily launched into a dissertation on her interpretation of what such words mean, all very matter-of-factly, as if the words' truths were in a bag that she had a firm grip on. What she handed me was the well-rehearsed spin, the dogmas of New Age spirituality. Whether it's organized religion or New Age spiritualism, dogma often reigns supreme, even if the dogma is anti-dogma. As I listened, I wondered if she really, truly believed it or just thought that was what she was supposed to say.

The idea of living a spiritual life often seems to come down to the idea that you must have some sort of practice or ideology or belief about God or the universe or both, and if you could throw in a unicorn and dolphins that would be awesome because, as we all know, they are very spiritual, as are most animals—except slugs. Take those off the list. I mean, what is the universe saying to me when I see a slug?

I like to spin mystical tales about nature to my children; we can spend hours of delight in talking about all God's creatures and how they have important purposes and meanings. The bees pollinate the plants, the flies break down the poop, and so on and so on. Nary a spider has been squished in our house for fear that we might accidently tip the balance of nature and somehow cause Armageddon. One time, my daughter, who had brought home a note from school about head lice, asked me,

"Mom, if all the creatures in the world have a special purpose and are magical, then please explain lice to me." That was a really good question.

Kids have this way of finding the hole in any argument and drilling at it until it's a cavern and you're at the bottom trying to climb out. Meanwhile, your kids just shake their heads at you, baffled by your failed attempts to make sense of something that just doesn't need to make sense. Then you say the words you thought you would never utter to your children: "Because I said so." I never thought I would use the words that left me so unsatisfied as a child, but I guess that's what happens to parents. One day you wake up, and you look into the eyes of your children and see yourself, and you look into a mirror and see your parents, and out pops stuff like *because I said so*.

I have sometimes revisited my inner five-year-old's exasperation when having conversations with people about spiritual stuff. Take the Law of Attraction, for example. This is a very complex, multilayered concept, which in our "fast food, make it easy for me in three steps, please, because I don't really have the time or the energy to dig to the core of this concept, I'll just take the CliffsNotes and run with it" world has been boiled down to the oversimplified idea that if you put out positive thoughts, good things (like cars) will come. I used to picture myself at Law of Attraction conventions wearing a t-shirt that says, *It's about the inside, people.* Seriously, how can the answer to anything be out there if it, by force of nature, is originating in here?

Many people seemed intent on having the kinds of conversations that debate stuff like whether hatha yoga is more spiritual than Bikram, whether we should be hot or cold or neither, and whether I must do yoga wearing lululemon or if any old sweat pants will do. Then there are the conversations on meditation. If you ever hear a New Ager start a conversation with the word meditation, run. I cannot count the number of times that I've been sucked into a debate on how meditation only works if you do it for three hours, not twenty minutes, or vice versa. Yet despite the wide range of opinions on how long to meditate, everyone always agrees that you must do it precisely right if you really want to reach that ever-elusive space called The Void (sounds ominous, right? Or is that just me?).

Why was I searching for a black hole with nothing in it, any-way? We have this incredible opportunity to experience a life filled with emotions and all that entails, but there were times when it felt like everyone was telling me I needed to learn how *not* to do any of that, that I should kill my ego, let go of attach-ment and the desire for nice things, and walk around smiling all the time.

If I didn't have a specific practice or ideology or belief about the nature of reality, could I not still be living a spiritual life? How can we decide what is spiritual and what isn't? In my head there is a committee answering all of this crap, and they stand in the big pasture in the sky and pick off cows, shouting, "This one is spiritual!" and "This one isn't! Put 'er down!"

All of these conversations made me stumble around. It was like getting directions from different people describing the same landmarks in drastically different ways, and I kept trying to orient myself to at least one thing. In the end, my point of reference became one basic thought: if everyone believes that what they believe is the real and correct spiritual universe and path, then all spirituality becomes correct. I think?

It would have been awesome if there had been just one road, made way back in the day, that we knew for sure was real and correct instead of a whole bunch of different roads leading to The Answer. Which I still do not have despite having taken a lot of freaking well-marked roads trying to find it.

I will admit, I'm lost. Yippee! Probably because I took the alternative scenic route and messed with my cows. I rearranged them for a while, as if the order they were in would somehow make it all click and cause happiness and peace light to finally appear on the horizon. That didn't happen, mostly because when you travel the less-used road, you end up stopping in unexpected places where you do unexpected things. Like tipping cows.

I wanted to know what would happen if instead of saying I'm living a spiritual life, I just said I'm alive, and that's pretty freaking spiritual. Or what if instead of picking one way, I didn't pick any way? Would I explode? And is it okay if I play the whole enlightenment and happiness thing by ear? Because, holy shit, keeping this smile going 24/7 is starting to hurt my face.

I had profound concerns about how livable spirituality was going to be for me if I had to first understand quantum physics, or HeartMath, or spiritual geometry, to meet the goal of being blissful all the time. Of course, since being blissful seemed to have deep connections to the endless-smiling thing, I also started to wonder about having that as an end game. Also, I have to say, I wasn't feeling the whole "forgive every asshole who broke your heart so you can finally be spiritual" philosophy.

And I was totally stumped by the idea of finding the right path when I didn't even know the right *me*.

But even with those thoughts popping in and out of my head, I just played along, never fully able to reconcile all the contradictions. I spent my time looking for wholeness, desperate to feel complete, and thinking something or someone was going to do that for me. I was also living in fear. I was afraid to say anything, and I was afraid to expose my inability to understand. I was afraid to admit I wasn't happy and afraid to say my life wasn't perfect. I feared that maybe I wasn't really very spiritual, and I feared that people might think I was stupid (big personal cow!).

After *What the Bleep Do We Know!?* came out and everyone decided I was somehow "in the know," I certainly wasn't going to let them down. One of my sacred-sacred cows was caring about what others thought of me. To be fair to myself, much of what I learned while making *Bleep* made a lot of sense. It worked in my life until it didn't, at which point I had no idea why it had stopped. I traversed the globe sharing ideas about how to live and be happy, how to attain enlightenment, even if deep down inside I didn't really know what that was or whether I even wanted it. As I did this, I saw the cracks in the ceramics but I often ignored them, especially when I saw that the other people who supposedly knew the answers also had cracks. I ignored them and, like a good student, put my nose to the ground and studied more and more and more, thinking that maybe the next thing would give me the answer.

I built my shelf[†] to store all the sacred cows I had gathered, and I tried to live all of them. I put on a great show of wisdom and understanding so that it appeared that I was "in the know" just like everyone else. Because I was afraid.

This was the state of me, from the time I was eight until that day when I was almost forty-one. My world was crashing down on top of me, with the endless contradictions disintegrating the ground I thought I had my feet firmly planted upon. The partial understandings I'd picked up along the way from others, most of whom also only partially understood, meant that my inner foundations sat upon sand, making everything shift and shake.

It took a while for me to remember that we're all afraid to show the cracks in our facades. I had forgotten that sometimes we all feel that not being perfect is somehow like the plague, and people are afraid it might rub off on them.

On that morning of The Epiphany, there were many moments of clarity mixed in with the sludge. The biggest ah-ha! I had was that I had been lying to myself and everyone I knew. As I began to clean off my cow-filled shelf, I decided that I was going to start with living authentically. I wasn't going to grab on to any idea, ideology, concept, or sacred cow unless it truly made sense to me, the real me. I let go of the idea that any one of those cows was the end all, be all. Those sacred cows would not bring me happiness. I promised myself that I would be honest with myself and others about how I was feeling, even if it meant admitting that sometimes my life sucked, that I had no idea what the meaning of life was, and that, in essence (and literally), my shit stank too. I promised myself that I would give myself a break and that I didn't always have to know.

I decided to take an unmarked route and have some fun exploring the sacred cows, not only in terms of spirituality (i.e., enlightenment, living in bliss, attachments), but also the sacred cows I had created about myself—my beliefs about who I was. I decided to forge my own path, one that might not always seem spiritual, but was, because everything is spiritual, at least to me. No separation needed.

Not having to decipher the "what is spiritual" code gave me the freedom to just be who I was from moment to moment—cigarette smoking, cocktail drinking, hot mama or contemplative, aware, spiritual chick (or both)—to know that no matter how I was feeling, what yoga pants I was wearing, it was okay. It was all, in fact, okay. And okay is good; okay is spiritual; okay is actually really awesome.

That is why I wrote this book. Because when I began to ask questions and dig deeper into the cows I had created, I found that a lot of people were thinking the same thing. Not just people who had only recently taken their first step on the "path," but many of my friends and colleagues who had been on it for years, people I thought had it all figured out. Suddenly, saying "I don't know" was cool.

I found that even the savviest of cow shoppers sometimes pick up more cows than they need. They overstuff their shelves too, and forget what's in the back hidden behind the latest and greatest.

Maybe it was because I decided it was okay to flail and fuck up and be lost that I could finally see others in my sphere going through the same thing. It felt like a sudden mutual event, where together we all heaved a collective sigh of relief that we didn't have to put on the show any longer, at least among ourselves. My path doesn't have to look like anyone else's, and it's cool if my way is different from yours. After reaching this conclusion, I began to really enjoy the contradictions, the multiple dimensions we all have. I learned that it's possible to be more than one thing at a time, that I could hang out with the vegans and not feel guilty because I was a killer of cows. I like meat, dammit, and I'm not going to rot in bovine hell for it. And I really started to like not knowing. It's nice to be able to accept the *sense* that an idea or concept has the weight of meaning without needing to dissect every last bit of why it seems like a weighty idea. I began to like the mystery of spiritual ambiguity.

That last one was hard. We are a society that likes answers, and in our plugged-in lives we often don't seem to care whether the answers illuminate the context of the question. Right or wrong, we want the unknown cleared away. We have lost the willingness to hang in the mystery. I know I certainly did. It feels pretty good to have it back.

And that is what I have written about here, because I want to offer you an invitation to regain your sense of the mystery, and to be okay with the spiritual flail, no matter how awkward you might feel on the dance floor. Each of the chapters in this book is my own tipping of a sacred cow (and sometimes the claiming of a sacred cow that I have decided to embrace, because we should do that too) I have created about life, spirituality, and everything in between. It's my own exploration into spirituality and what I've come to understand about it, and whether and how I use it in my life.

A little thing about perspectives: guess what—I have one, and it's mine, all mine. This doesn't mean it's right; it just means that this is one way of looking at things that might be of interest. I share stories from my past and in those stories are other people, most notably my ex-husband and my kids, none of whom have been given a chance to verbalize their own perspective in this book. The reason for that is that, well, this is my book, and therefore it is my perspective on them, the events we shared together, and what I learned from them. That, in turn, is a very important cow to be able to tip, the basic understanding and *accepting* that you have a perspective and that's all it is.

I've spent some time in these pages breaking down some of the big sacred cows of spirituality, hoping you'll walk away with a different perspective of their meanings, or at least an idea of what they mean to me. Read the chapters in order or on their own. But remember to laugh, because that's one cow I won't be tipping. Being able to laugh and let go of being so serious about everything, in my humble experience, is the ultimate sacred cow, the kind you hold on to like hell.

Notes

* I was also baffled by the need for separate churches. Why all these different versions? I mean, if the Bible was a factual historical record, how come there were so many different interpretations? And some of the rules seemed a little incongruous to my young self: God loves and forgives, but Jesus needed to die for our sins; love your neighbor, but not if he's gay; don't kill, but kill if they don't believe; have a personal relationship with God, but pray in public places. Holy crap! Talk about your mixed messages. And what's up with the conflation of Old Testament stuff with New Testament stuff? So confusing!

† So, yes, I realize that the sacred cows are now, metaphorically speaking, simultaneously in a pasture and also on this shelf. I could say that it is a

slight tip of my hat to quantum physics and the awesomeness that is the electron, but alas, I only thought of that right now as I was justifying my metaphor two-timing. In reality, I just like using metaphors and wanted to mix it up with the sacred-cow-pasture thing. Meta, meta, meta. This is all painfully self-aware. Argh! It never stops . . .

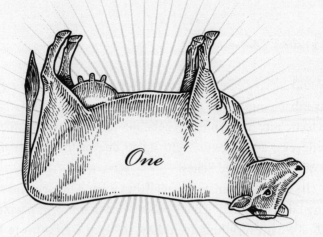

One

Red Shirts in Your Brain

Imagine you've lived in a big city all your life. You've traveled the world; hell, you've even had sex almost underneath the Eiffel Tower (okay, the hotel room had an awesome view—pay no never mind to the fact that I was looking at the view while having sex). So what's next? For me it was Yelm, Washington. Yep, that's right. After the semi-okay, not so big, big O with a view of the epitome of romance, what else would a girl do?

When I moved to rural Washington, I found a small redneck town that was supposedly the only spot on the planet that would survive when the waters swelled, drowning the earth and its inhabitants in the days of Armageddon. Yelm is home to an eclectic mix of spiritual seekers, fundamentalist Christians, and rednecks, and it butts right up to one of the largest military bases in the United States.

It's a small town, really small, but it has a library, and not just any library—imagine trying to service that mix of people! That library has everything from how to clean your guns to how to store food for the end of the world (and why are we saving food if the world's going to end? Note to self: follow up—try to answer). The other thing that serviced the eclectic populace of Yelm was the rain, which it did, almost every day. Between the rain and the lack of anything resembling something to do, because a girl can only garden and can vegetables for so many hours in a day, the Yelm library is the place to go.

I regularly took my daughter there when she was younger, initiating her into the cult of stories, books, and reading, which libraries are indubitably perfect for, being, as they are, a place for learning, for absorbing words and the meaning of things, with stacks of stories and knowledge just waiting to be explored. And boy, do we humans love our stories. And did I mention it rained, a lot!

On one particular trip, we had done all the things we normally did. We started by reading stories about birds sitting on heads and scared squirrels. From there we played with the broken library toys—you know, the puzzles with missing pieces and the stuffed toys that have just seen too much love (as if that's possible). The toys that make you want to sanitize every inch of yourself with wipes after you get back in your car because they are all a little bit sticky and you can practically see the layers of kid-carried germs all over them.

After we were sufficiently sticky and our minds were filled with stories of bears and caterpillars, we ambled toward the door, my daughter chattering at me as she skipped along, her little hand in mine, while I made sounds of agreement and attention. As we approached the door, in walked one of her little friends from school. A beautiful little girl, along with her equally beautiful mother.

I am great at doing that thing people do, where we catalogue another person in the blink of an eye, run a list of comparisons, and judge by a predetermined set of conditions who is better, happier, and sexier. I did this, standing in the library, in the blink of an eye. Let me add that the woman I was comparing myself to, in my compare and contrast throw-down, had all the qualities I yearned for—long legs, a perfect body, and gorgeous cheekbones. These are things that used to and, sigh, sometimes still do, feed my self-image propaganda sponge of all things that destroy good thoughts about myself. This propaganda sponge is the reason I describe myself, somewhat regularly, as short and stout.

So compare and contrast I did, standing there as my daughter danced around me. Guess who won in my little head battle? Hint-hint, it wasn't the short and stout one. The deciding factor, the thing that really brought home the other mother's win? I knew she was one of those baby-body-rebounders. Pregnant one minute, on the runway the next.

I have, in my past (and sometimes in my now), had a secret hatred of women who can give birth and have their body back within an hour. Mostly because I had no such luck.

Prior to getting pregnant, when I lived on a steady diet of Diet Coke and cigarettes, I happily fit into size-one jeans. My thought was that my skinniness would make up for my lack of inches in the height department. However, no matter how thin I was, no amount of dieting ever reduced the size of my ass. It came, it was, it stayed.

Even at a size one, I still had what my mother affectionately referred to as birthing hips. Thanks, Mom. My brother doubled down on my mom's description (because it was so awesome) by referring lovingly to me as his little hippo—I shit you not, this happened without them ever clueing in to the idea that their words might not be flattering. So I picked up some baggage there and carried it around on my hips and ass.

After I gave birth to my daughter and the weight did not drop off like I had hoped it would, I built an image and a story in my head that helped me feel better about hanging on to those extra pounds. My daughter and I were both happy and healthy, and we would grow out of our baby weight together. It wasn't until I was confronted with the perfect little waif children and their equally perfectly proportioned mothers that my projected story stung.

▌   ▌   ▌

Standing in the library, I did the comparison, and I found myself lacking, all without being aware of it, ingrained and imbedded as these things are. I exchanged the mandatory and cursory hello, and I asked my daughter if she wanted to stay for a bit longer. She squeaked with excitement, as if playing with

Mom was okay but playing with another person her size was pure heaven.

So back we headed to the kiddie section. The other mother and I exchanged smiles, realizing we could possibly check out some grown-up books or maybe, God forbid, have a grown-up conversation while our little angels delighted in the merriments only four-year-olds can truly understand. The library was pretty contained, so I snuck around the corner to take a peek at the magazines. I could hear piping little girl voices, deciding what to do, what to read. "Oh, look at this book," said the little friend. "I love this stuffy," said mine, holding tightly to the overloved bear we had just parted ways with not five minutes ago. Man, did she love that bear, slight stickiness and all.

Surrounded by storybooks, the girls built their conversation, talking about the things that young children understand to be important and that adults have, probably stupidly, turned away from. I heard the friend say something that struck me. "You look like you're pregnant, ya know. You're fat." And in a moment that went by faster than the speed of light, I heard a sob, not just any sob, but the sob of a four-year-old who has so much pain and doesn't even understand why. The voice of my brother echoed in my head: "Hi, hippo girl." I dropped my magazine and with the speed of a mother lion had my daughter wrapped in my arms as she cried uncontrollably.

I knew that this was one of those carry-with-you-all-your-life moments for her. I could hear in the hurt of her sobs that the moment and the words had crawled inside and shifted basic elements of how she viewed the world and herself. I knew in that moment that no words of mine could undo it. Time could not move backward and unsay what my child had heard.

Is this, I wondered, how it starts? Whammo, and for the rest of her life she will always wonder: Am I fat? Am I beautiful? Just like I have.

∎   ∎   ∎

This moment for my daughter made me think of my own moments, those I can point to and say, "Wow. That changed me hugely." There are little moments too, like when you decided that the color green just wasn't as much your color as blue, or when you decided on a preference for lilies over roses. When you decided that the right side of the bed rocked and the left side felt strange. When you decided your eyebrows were too close together and your nose was too pointy.

This concept fascinates me. It makes me want to hunt down where and when all of my choices, reactions, and beliefs, big and small, came from. It makes me want to pull a Sherlock Holmes on everyone else too. Why do you like socks so much? Elementary, dear boy. When you were very little you wore a pair that had Santa on them. It was the same year you got your favorite present ever, and you've liked socks ever since.

My fascination with the how, why, and what of our thinking has not been a transitory thing for me. I have, in my search to figure out myself and understand others, explored a great deal. What I have found has helped me, greatly and in surprising ways. In order to start from the beginning of my current under-standing of The Way Things Work (capitalized for me, because this is a belief—a sacred cow—that I have now chosen to hold as true), we have to really start from the beginning, as in birth.

We are made of moments, starting at the moment we pop out of the uterus and begin our lives here on Earth. We unconsciously attach meanings to everything as a normal function of our brains. Everything has to mean something, right? Both simple and complex: red lights mean stop, green lights mean go, and apples mean sin, smart, food, America (via pie), teaching, and learning. Simple and complex.

Our brains are marvelous things. Hell, we are marvelous things, in our sponge-ish ways, when it comes to the info gathering. From our mother's first snuggle, to the first time we feel fear, to our first love, and on and on, we take it all in. It's what we do. It's how the human system works, and that's pretty much it. Or is it? Cue dramatic music.

Like I said, our brains are amazing because, like Ginsu knives, they can do all of that and more. We can also interrupt that process with conscious input. We can even interrupt the brain's process long enough to decide whether or not we want to believe something (What?! Why didn't I think of that before I decided to believe I was a hippo? Foiled!). This is a big assertion, no doubt about it. Mostly because we are complex and have layers. We are semantics rich. This makes it hard to pin things down.

But we do have choices about how we decide to label and accept a moment. Knowing this, I have discovered, is the difference between spending our lives making choices based on old beliefs and meanings we have unconsciously attached to things—meanings that have become so ingrained they stop us from actually having any new ideas, interpretations, or experiences that could lead us in a new direction—and taking a moment to choose whether we want that belief or not. If we don't assess our beliefs, our future is almost certainly predictable. All we have to do is look backward.

And who wants a future that's simply based on the past?

Apparently I did, because every time I looked in a mirror, all I saw was a six-year-old hippo—short legs with big hips and sometimes even a big mouth to go with them. And because I believed with every ounce of my being that I was a hippo, all I saw was a hippo.

I realized pretty much right away that if I was going to tip over my sacred cows—my beliefs about who I was and how the world worked—and consciously create my future, I should probably start by understanding how I picked them up in the first place. All the old patterns and unconscious belief systems needed to be exposed. Yeah, right, I'll just let go of that belief I've held on to for the majority of my life like a three-year-old with a dedicated blankie. Have you ever tried to take away your three-year-old's blankie at an airport security checkpoint? I think disarming North Korea would probably be easier. Sometimes this is how we feel about the meanings and beliefs we have collected. Even if they constantly derail us, we like them, we know them, and just like that blankie, all sticky and smelling like stale milk, no one is going to take them away from us.

I like to know how things work. I like a plan, a process, sort of a road map; if I know how I got there, then I can probably get back home. It's easier to change if I know what the process of adopting beliefs is about in the first place. And the first place it starts is in the brain.

Let's start by going over how the brain gets into certain habits. There are literally hundreds of great books about this. My favorite is neuroscientist Dr. Joe Dispenza's *Breaking the Habit of Being Yourself*, which I highly recommend. But here, without going into great detail, are the basics. I promise, you won't have to be a neuroscientist to get it.

Dr. Joe tells us "cells that fire together, wire together."[1] Well, he isn't kidding. Our brains, you know, that enormously complex three pounds of blobby stuff in our heads, are made up of about 90,000 miles of fibers; that's the same length as the shoreline in all of Minnesota—a trivia gift, from me to you. With all that real estate, we have the ability to absorb information quickly and efficiently. As we get older and the beliefs and meanings we have picked up along the way become tried and true, we're less likely to try to teach that blob upstairs anything new. That old saying about teaching an old dog new tricks? It's mostly true. Think about how often you repeat a behavior or a pattern with the same outcome. Even though you know you're going to get the same results, you do it again anyway! Now imagine how often you do that without even being conscious of it.

The beliefs and meanings we have picked up along the way are now tried and true. At least we think they are. Our learned beliefs reside in the neurons of our brains, and they are triggered at the synaptic level, the little junction between neurons where information is relayed like little sparks. When we learn something, neural synapses fire with other associated neurons and their synapses and whammo! Lights go off, similar information hooks up, and meaning is attached. If there is emotion involved when we have an experience (and when isn't an emotion involved?), the information is impressed deeply into our subconscious. Stay with me here; it sounds more complicated than it is.

All of this is happening every nanosecond of our lives without us really paying attention to the process or even knowing it's happening. Sort of like breathing—you just do it, no need to think about how you do it. But knowing how this one process works can make the difference between being truly happy or kind of, sort of not—between living life or life living you.

Let's say you're a hypothetical baby, to give a bare bones example of a complex system, and you're on a walk with your mom. You're hanging out in your stroller, gumming that weird squishy thing given to you by the Big Being with the boobs you love to snuggle. You look up at the Boob Being and suddenly you feel this odd sensation, and it doesn't feel good. Boob Being looks scared, and because you're so sensitive, you pick up her emotions and then you feel scared (you don't know it's fear, but you know you don't like the feeling!). Suddenly, as if from nowhere (hey, you're a baby, things appear and disappear like magic because you're somewhat shortsighted and also because your brain doesn't "get" all the information it is receiving yet), another Big Being in a bright red shirt rushes past you, bumping into the Boob Being, and she recoils with a cry. BOOM! Sparks fly! Neurons ignite! And guess what? Your hypothetical baby brain has just created a belief that big man beings in red shirts are scary. Because of all the emotion involved, you unconsciously decide to store that one away in your subconscious because you think you're probably going to need that information. You won't realize why, but for the rest of your life you will have a subconscious fear of men in red shirts. Our brains are awesome, even when they red-shirt you.

It happens in a nanosecond, and as we grow, those meanings become attached to other meanings. Neurons link to other neurons, and soon a story is built up in our heads.

When we are really young and strangers in grocery stores comment on how adorable we are, that is the vision we hold of ourselves; that is what we believe about ourselves. How can we not, with the constant marveling of our family and their friends at our ability to crawl and say "Mama" or "Dada." The overly excited oohs and ahs at our scribbles on paper, as if we've outdone Picasso, fill us with a sense of pride about ourselves. It makes us feel empowered, beautiful, and even magnificent.

This same mechanism, the one that imbeds experiential magnificence in us, can mess with us too. I wasn't chubby as a baby, but somewhere around six or seven my body just stopped proportionately getting taller, so I started getting wider. I didn't really notice this until I began acting in commercials and those "how adorable" comments seemed to be fewer and farther in between.

The view of myself, my six-year-old's sense of being awesome in all ways, began to change when a casting director for a commercial passed me by for being "too chubby." It changed even more when a wardrobe woman called me "ill proportioned." With each of these moments, a feeling of hatred for my body was reinforced without my being conscious of it. The moment my brain recognized that the feedback paradigm had shifted from positive to critical, it began its work, making connections and moving perceptions. My brain then added those connections and perceptions to a thousand big and little moments that it had catalogued and built meaning around, until my belief about who I was began a slow nosedive into a pit of self-judgment and insecurity.

The same thing happened when my four-year-old daughter was told she looked pregnant. Synapses fire, and we carry that uncertainty about our bodies into every experience of our lives. We were red-shirted and, voilà, Hippo Girl is born.

My body image (dressed in a red shirt) followed me into adulthood. Trying on clothes could send me into a tailspin of doubt. When I asked, "Does this make me look fat?" it was a serious question, on the level of fate-of-the-world serious. I avoided shopping with friends because I was so embarrassed about my body. I had fat, dammit, and I needed to be alone with it. Short, chubby—nothing ever fit right. And the story in my head about my body only grew worse after having kids. I found myself buying clothes that screamed, "This woman has red-shirt issues!" They were all clothes that helped make me feel worse about myself. When I got them home, I would stand in front of my mirror, rolling up the bottom of my jeans because they never seem to make jeans with legs short enough and hips wide enough to fit right. Then I'd tug on my billowing pirate shirt—you know, the kind that's supposed to hide your love handles (who ever coined that term had a mean streak)—hearing the word *hippo* chanted over and over again in my head and trying to remember why I had thought these looked good on me in the store.

What finally changed how I dressed myself was a TV show on TLC. Spending a quiet Saturday without my kids, I was wandering around in my head, seriously not knowing what to do with myself, when it dawned on me that there was this thing called a TV and that people other than my children could use it. I figured I'd indulge in a little mind numbing because, having experienced what watching it does to my children, I assumed that was what it was for.

I ciphered the remote control and flipped on the TV, victorious over the serious technology now employed to turn the power on and switch some freaking channels. I flipped through for a while before I stumbled upon a show called *What Not to Wear*. As silly as it might sound, that show changed me. There was a woman on the show who looked a lot like me. I listened as the hosts explained what types of clothes she should be buying, and I was surprised. I thought, well, shit, that's me. Wow, forty-mumble-mumble years on this planet, and I never considered that it wasn't me or my body that was the problem—it was the types of clothes I was buying. Years of seriously not liking my body, and I could have simply changed the style and cut of the clothes I wore.

This epiphany eluded me for years, all because someone once told me I was short and fat, and short and fat people can't wear nice clothes because nice clothes aren't made for people with that kind of body. I considered how those wardrobe people, the ones who were supposed to be experts about clothes, could have saved me a lot of pain if they'd given me some advice instead of just pointing out my chubby thighs.

Well, you know what? Screw you, casting and wardrobe ladies from my past, and screw you too, fucking red-shirted cow. You may think that the girl can't fit the clothes, but I finally know it just isn't true!

Once I began to play with the "it's not me, it's the clothes" concept, I started to see great things about my body. I've got great legs. They're short, but shapely! My shoulders are gorgeous! I have a great smile and beautiful eyes! The confidence that my six-year-old self once had began to wake up. Suddenly the little things about my body that I wasn't so proud of didn't matter. And even though I still don't wear a bikini, I love going to the beach with my kids, because I accept that I am a beautifully flawed human in a beautifully flawed body. I worked hard to gain some of those bumps, and if I really want to, I can work hard (and sweat a little) to get rid of them. And some of them are here to stay, but they don't define me.

It was also painfully clear to me that it wasn't only that moment in the library that had made an impression on my daughter. She was also paying close attention to me, to my sense of body, to my feelings about what I saw in the mirror, from how I dressed to how I hid. I noticed she liked baggy clothes that hid her figure, just like I did. Not only was it important for me to find love for my body for myself, it was important for her too.

It sounds a lot easier reading it here. Like I just changed my mind. Actually, that is indeed what I did, but the tipping of this cow took some time and some work. It took practice and patience and a commitment to interrupting the pattern ingrained in my old hippo self. The brain makes you work for it. It didn't take much for me to believe I was short and fat and ugly, but it did take work for me to teach myself a new belief.

Before I could even begin said journey of appreciation of my body, I first had to let go of old beliefs and pain. I had to stop allowing someone else's opinions to become my truth, and I had to stop clinging to past meanings that simply weren't true. I had to have some serious heart-to-hearts with myself until my brain started to make different connections. Easier said than done, I know.

I still work on it, pretty much every day, it seems. It is especially tough since most (if not all) of our beliefs have come from the people we surround ourselves with. They are people we love, people we admire, or think we should admire, even people we are afraid of or hesitant about, and we suck their beliefs in like Hoover vacuum cleaners.

It's something we seem to forget, that pretty much everyone we encounter is walking around with their own beliefs, which they share all willy-nilly. It's because we're all so good with the sharing, what with having been told since we were little to share, share, share! Seriously, share stuff like chocolate and toys; keep your meme-y* beliefs to yourself if they aren't of the helpful variety.

And let's not forget about the media shoveling tons of fun things at us. Here's a fun fact—when I was a child actress, I did about twenty-five Mattel Barbie commercials. Have you ever seen those little girls on Barbie commercials? They are damn cute, aren't they? Never a hair out of place, not a spot on their clothes, and perfect little smiles. My perfect smile cost about ten grand to keep up. I had special temporary teeth for when I was missing one and had a commercial to do because God forbid other kids should see kids on television missing teeth like they do. This is how it starts, people, when you're six, all sweaty and covered in fruit juice, lisping along to the Oscar Meyer song. Try explaining to your seven-year-old that Selena Gomez isn't twelve, she's twenty, and that is why her body is fully developed, and she has about forty people running around behind her, brushing her hair, fixing her makeup, and picking out the perfect wardrobe that this mother just can't afford.

Sometimes our friends, even when they think they are being helpful, can be the worst white elephant gift givers. When I walked past my daughter's door one morning as we all prepared for our day, I overheard her and a friend discussing what she should wear to school. I heard her friend, who is the exact opposite of my daughter (funny how often we find friendships in people we wish we looked like, feeding into our body envy), say something about how my daughter couldn't wear jeans. Hearing my daughter and her friend talk, I heard the voices of my past telling me what was wrong with my body instead of finding things that were right.

Beliefs are learned in innumerable ways, often from one-off experiences like the baby and the red shirt, or from ideas handed to us over time. We learn beliefs from our parents or caregivers, our friends, TV, music, and, in my case, casting directors and wardrobe mistresses. We are built to take in data, to assess, label, and categorize. This helped us survive when we were the new hominids on the block, looking for the best possible outcome, the best possible bang for our effort, like couponers trying to make the most out of every possible coupon combo.

Humans love a good bargain, and there's nothing like grabbing a belief off someone else's shelf. I mean, it's free, right? They've done all of the initial work. Might as well make a copy so you can be twinsies. If my best friend says it, it must be true, and I'll say it too. Snagging someone else's beliefs, meanings, and understandings is something we do very well. The skill set of taking on knowledge, not from our own untainted-by-opinion experiences but from things learned by another, is a very human one. We build ourselves while standing on the shoulders of those who laid the groundwork before us. Imagine, if you will, what would happen to our civilization if we each individually had to learn and invent every bit of our individual knowledge, solo through our own discovery process. Imagine having to rediscover geometry every time we needed to build a bridge instead of learning it from our learned-knowledge history. That would suck, not to mention how tough it would make travel (especially since we'd probably be doing it on horseback).†

The thing I have learned is that our propensity for adopting others' knowledge, understandings, meanings, and beliefs is wonderful, but also dangerous and something to navigate with care. I have also learned that it can kind of make you brain-lazy. It's so much easier to have something handed to us prelabeled. Especially if we've heard it before and it matches the beliefs we already carry. We don't have to go through as many neuron stations to build our picture, because our picture has already been built for us. Of course the easiest thing, even easier than learning someone else's learning, is to simply go back into the brain computer and pull out the file that says "red shirt bad."

It is way easier to react unconsciously to all of it than to pause and take a moment not to react according to old impressions: the colors, the smells, the words. The brain likes repetition and having well-labeled, pre–figured-out things to easily reference. The same, the known, even when it hurts, somehow feels safer to us than the unknown, even if the unknown is where so many possibilities lie.

Realizing we are this way, that I am this way but I can change the situation, is probably the single most important lesson I have learned in my entire life. By understanding how my brain works, instead of allowing my brain and its subconscious programs to run amok on their own, I take charge. Yes, we humans like to think we know the truth even if it's untrue! And once we've decided it's truth, even if it's false, it's hard to change. But somewhere along the way, hopefully, we look in our belief closet and realize there's something amiss and it's time for a garage sale.

After my divorce, I realized that after forty-some odd years on this planet, I had picked up a whole lot of stuff I just didn't need and had made some pretty sacred beliefs for myself. They were beliefs of all varieties, from spiritual to body-image stuff, from cultural to political, from chocolate to panna cotta, things that I protected and refused to shift for fear of losing something. Beliefs that might have fit at one point or another, but no longer made me look so good.

So I began to get rid of them, slowly.

There are lots of ways to figure out what beliefs you have. Some people do regression therapy or go to meditation retreats to get a handle on their baggage, but I prefer the practical approach and use lists and observation. I spend time observing my reactions to things, my feelings and opinions about a situation. I allow myself time to go through every thought because shoving thoughts away, simply ignoring them, and judging them before they've had time to be expressed, just leaves them to fester like rotting meat in the compost pile. You don't want meat in your compost pile.

I organize my lists into categories depending on whether my responses are reasonable or emotional and based on old beliefs. The methodical nature of making lists is, for me, an easy way to clean out my closet. If it's reasonable, then I can explore a reasonable response. If it's emotional baggage, it gets tipped. I also play a game I call My Life Sucks. It's dramatic and fun and heart wrenching, but it works for me (I have included it in the appendix so you can play it too).

When I dug deep into my beliefs, I found most of them were connected to the concept of worthiness: I wasn't pretty so I wasn't worthy of love; I wasn't smart because I didn't go to college and therefore wasn't worthy of success; and so on. I am going to go out on a limb here and make a grand statement: my guess is that, especially for women, most of our beliefs about ourselves are connected to worthiness. Our view of our self-worth makes a lot of decisions for us about the life we are going to live—at least it did in my case. Drilling down to that core understanding has made a huge impact on me. It's why I am able to sit here and write this book. I actually believe that what I have to say has value to other people. Imagine that. The short, chubby, dumb girl has something to say. Why, yes, yes I do.

This understanding of why I believe what I believe about myself and the world I live in is the cornerstone of my work these days. It's not so much based in "spirituality" as it is based in the science of how this body, this tool I've been given to experience the world I'm in, is used. This is my foundation for picking and choosing the beliefs I take with me on my continued journey. Because before I can decide what is spiritual, before I can decide who I want to be, I need to understand what I believe I am.

With practice I, and anyone, can interrupt those old patterns and begin to build new ones. As Dr. Joe Dispenza has said many times, it takes repetition. Just like hearing "hippo" and "chubby" all my life, I needed to start hearing how beautiful I was, starting with telling it to myself. To do this, I built my own bullshit meter. My little game My Life Sucks is played often, sometimes in a speed round, in the nanoseconds between breaths. Before I decide to take on a new belief, I listen to the inner voice that is a guru and a friend. And if I don't have time for a speed round, I simply wait until I do. We don't have to decide right then and there if we need that shiny new belief. Sometimes there is a peace that comes with sleeping on it.

That day when my daughter was given a belief, a meaning she had not chosen, my heart broke for my beautiful girl. My heart broke for all us little girls. It will be years before she is able to choose to change how she might react to what she was given. Hopefully all my yammering on about how her brain works, how beliefs get all jumbled up, and my constant reminders of her beauty will eventually sink in.

It took me until my forties, with an epiphany wrapped in a crisis, to finally understand how I worked. Even though it was hard and often painful, I don't regret it. We learn when we learn.

My take away is that I don't have to buy it, but if I do, I can return it. I can undo the neural connection with practice, just like I clean my desktop on my computer. I do it often, and instead of being something painful and arduous, it's sort of like Christmas every time I play. I get rid of what I don't want, find things I didn't know I had, and make room for change.

Notes

* A quick info dump on trendy memes, which are a little different from cultural meme-memes, both on the internet and out and about among actual physical people. They are also insanely easy to pick up—like the yearly flu. We are infected with little transient memes (think about the crazy explosion of "that's hot." Reality television was patient X, with an R-Naught of a bazillion. It was inescapable) against our will because our brains are built to actually be the bestest meme hosts ever. That train left the station when evolution decided cognitive cooperation was the way to go. There's a metaphor for memes that uses genes as an analogy and the idea of memes being "selected" into sticking within a culture or slipping away as a meme-dead end, i.e., trending or faddish memes.

† Meme me up, Scotty. We cannot escape replication of cultural stuff. It's in our cultural chromosomes, diligently passing on the pieces of stuff that makes us, us.

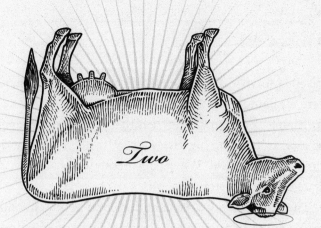

Enlightenment Says, Huh?

I once sat on a plane next to a young Buddhist monk. We struck up a conversation, and I learned he was traveling home after being in Burma for several years. He was originally from Laguna Beach and had left his silver-spooned, surfboarded upbringing for a simpler life. He had decided that seeking connection to his higher self and being free from the trappings of his consumer-driven life was the way to go.

We were sitting in coach, stuffed in with people traveling home, traveling toward vacation, traveling for work, and traveling to visit. Traveling toward and from—that is what we were all doing—and because people traveling on planes share this simple commonality, there is that instant connection where we look around and say, *Hey, look, we're all in this together*, and form an insta-tribe. Which apparently equals permission to share stories with strangers.

The young monk was smooth shaven with a smooth, bald head, and perhaps owing to the abundance of smoothness, he could have been any age between twenty and forty. His congeniality was positively evangelical in its sincerity. It made me want to be him or do whatever he was doing to achieve such an isn't-life-wonderful glow.

When the captain's disembodied voice announced we had reached our cruising altitude of thirty thousand feet, the monk apparently felt that we were elevated enough for him to talk about his spiritual journey. He shared his stories of fasting for enlightenment, trekking through the Himalayas for enlightenment, and spending months in silence, seeking the wisdom of the cosmos (for enlightenment, I assume). I was pretty impressed; I can't sit in silence for ten minutes, let alone for months at a time. He emanated a feeling of pure love and sereneness (plus congeniality), and he had that little monk laugh as if everything were funny. It said, "I am truly living in bliss."

As the plane landed and the rest of us zombies—the shuffling masses lost in an illusion the monk seemed to have risen above—dug at our feet for our collection of material comforts, I half expected him to float off the plane, never touching the ground. Anticlimactically, that didn't happen. Instead we said our good-byes, and he ambled away, high-top Keds peeking out from under his robes.

I made my way down to baggage claim, following the arrows that pointed vaguely in a general direction—you know, like when it could either be pointing toward the escalator or the hallway that continues past the escalator. Those vague markers that point toward several choices when all you want is one clearly delineated, correct path toward your luggage, are about the most annoying things in an airport. Just tell me exactly which way to go, please, so I can get the crap I need to continue on with my life. And, yes, there is a possible analogy to be made there, but not yet, as this was before I knew enough to notice I was in the middle of a metaphor.

The baggage claim areas in airports are always interesting places to watch people spaz, just a little. First, you never know if you are at the right carousel because the scroll board isn't updated by the time you get there, so you have no confirmation that you are actually where you are supposed to be. So there you are, standing next to a nonmoving conveyer belt, surreptitiously looking at everyone around you to see if you recognize anyone from your flight. Second, there is the anxiety of waiting for your luggage once the conveyer belt has started—what if it didn't make the plane? But really, there is an odd limbo-ness in baggage claim; it is both a destination and a stopover to a later destination. Limbo indeed.

There I was, a zombie, standing in limbo, looking around surreptitiously to see if I was with my plane-tribe, and there he was again, the smooth monk, standing with a cart and waiting for his luggage. It dawned on me that maybe it was odd for a

Buddhist monk to be waiting in baggage claim, because wasn't not having stuff kind of the point? Then, rousing from my zombie stupor, I watched the utter absurdity of this little man fighting gallantly to pull not one, not two, but three Tumi suitcases off the conveyer belt. And these weren't the imitation Tumi either. These were designer—steel, with the four wheels that go in all directions. Very fancy for a monk. Hell, they were fancy for me and everyone I know. The moment totally tickled my irony bone.

I watched, delighted with the incongruity, as he muscled the luggage onto his cart and headed for the door. I gathered my fully realized, and fully cheap, Walmart duffel bag and headed for the curb myself. And there he was, yelling into a cell phone: "Mom, I told you I was landing at three today, not tomorrow. God dammit!"

I decided I could take trekking through the Himalayas off my list in my search for enlightenment, because clearly it wasn't hiding there.

The monk's stories about his spiritual journey to find enlightenment and my own journey to baggage claim and what it illuminated in a different way made me think about my own enlightenment in general. Could I really *do* what I thought enlightenment *meant*? Could I really walk away from everything in my life just so I could live in perpetual lightness and bliss? I couldn't imagine my kids thinking an orange robe was enough clothing, a shaved head was a good look, or that eating only one bowl of soup once a day was awesome. Would it be worth it? Was it possible to be enlightened and still have a life? What was enlightenment, and did I want it?

I I I

I find that sometimes getting back to the basics, digging down to the core of a concept and gaining clarity about its meaning, helps me know exactly what it is I am seeking so that I may actually find it. In order to do that, I think it's important to understand the origins of the terminology, to figure out where the philosophies and ideas came from and what their original meaning was. If I understand what it really means, then I can decide if, in fact, it is really what I seek.

Not unlike modern organized religions, much of modern Western spirituality has been pulled from many different sources. People have pulled a little from here, a little from there, so that our sensibilities can accept and make sense of spirituality in the lives we live, which are vastly different from the lives of the people who originally undertook such noble paths. I (probably) would not be willing to go through some of the practices the ancients' schools of wisdom used to put their young disciples through. Think pits of snakes and starvation. Just say no.

Many ancient schools and traditions had very specific practices and steps to guide followers along the path. Now, with the hodgepodge of mix-and-match spirituality, it's easy to become lost in the quagmire, falling deep into the rabbit hole. This can sometimes be a good thing, but often we just end up more lost and confused, frustrated at ourselves and the world around us. Mainly because we're not even sure of what we're looking for or if we really want it.

A lot of the time, when we take our firsts step onto the "spiritual" path, when we ask those first questions, the idea of enlightenment is held out before us as the illustrious piece of cheese at the end of the maze. It seems like the pinnacle of all we are searching for, and we spend our lives wandering through corridors, salivating, endlessly turning from one hallway to the next, the smell of that cheese driving us forward. Once you're enlightened, you've arrived! But . . .

What is enlightenment?

Etymologically speaking, the English word *enlightenment* is actually a word with other word elements hooked on: *en*, *light*, *en* again (a different meaning from a different root), and *ment*. We can kind of follow the course of its arrival and attendant meaning into our modern Western understanding by starting with the word *light*.

The root of *enlightenment* comes from a very old (think Dark Ages) noun form of the word *light*. We find it in the Old English word *leoht*, which is related to the Old Saxon and Old High German word *lioht*, which more than likely had congress with the Goth *liuhap*, all of which mean brightness, radiant energy, luminous, and beautiful. Not that anyone was focusing on light in the Dark Ages, but I digress.

From there, our Dark Age word makers hitched on an *en*, to get *lighten*, which started as *nian*, and also originated from Old English usage. *En/nian* was a word bit whose sole point of existence was to be added to a noun or adjective to make it take action, making the noun *light* into the verb *lighten*, and so *light* gets to shed light upon, illuminate, and brighten. Apparently, at some point between the first and fourteenth centuries (I'm guessing 1066—think the Norman invasion of the British Isles), this verbing of light did not conceptually say what it was trying to say strongly enough, because the word-intensifier *en* from the Old French was added. *En* had been pulled into the Old French from a previous relationship with the Latin *in*, which means *in* or *into*. And so *en* and *lighten* became BFFs.

We have now arrived at *enlighten*, which is really a way of saying "to seriously shed light, super-duper illuminate, and hella-brighten," which is pretty cool. And it's actually double cool because structurally, the preposition-ness of the Old French *en*/Latin *in*, meaning *in* and *into*, infers the idea that we are *inside* or *moving inside* the action of shedding light upon something. It is the sense of being inside it, not just acting on it, that intensifies the meaning. Being inside the action means we are entirely *being* the thing we are *doing*. Deep.

The figurative sensibility of *enlighten* was further developed while still in its Old English form *inlihtan*, and it came to mean "to remove dimness or blindness from one's eyes or heart." This shift into symbolic meaning was more than likely from the truly epic connection made by the Church between godliness and the concept of *light*.

At some point, as Old English swung into a more modern version of itself, the word *enlighten* met up with a renewed interest in the teachings of the old philosophers—you know, Plato and other contemplative dead dudes—and the action of removing dimness to illuminate became a "something" to attain, a "someplace" to be. So they added the suffix *ment*, from the Latin *mentum*, which indicates that the word it is attached to is now a result or product of the action it used to be. In short, the noun *light* became the verb *lighten* and then to intensify it, it became an even stronger sense of the verb by becoming *enlighten* and then it was shifted again, and the verb once more became a noun as *enlightenment* was born. We went from something that is to something that does, then back to something that is, but with more panache.

But I still have no idea what that something is, even if it is cooler and improved.

In the Western New Age or New Thought movement, the words *enlightenment* and *enlightened* have been thrown around more than a football on Thanksgiving. Everyone is talking about it, everyone's looking for it, but do you know anyone who has actually found it? Yeah, me neither.

I admit it: I got caught in the frenzied search for that illustrious hunk of cheese, reading every book and walking over every coal, thinking that one day I would suddenly go poof and ascend into masterdom, levitate magically into the realm of the gods, and hang out with the other enlightened, cool people. I've done a whole slew of random and even bizarre things in the name of becoming enlightened. Sadly, the "random" and "bizarre" part of that is not hyperbole. I've spent hours blindfolded, walking a football field and searching a fence as I looked for a card on which I had previously drawn a picture. The picture was supposed to represent what I wanted to manifest in my life, so if I wanted a Rolls Royce, I drew a picture of it, and if I miraculously found my card after hours of searching blindfolded, I should be able to walk out into the parking lot and find my fancy new car—spoiler alert, I never found the card and the new car never happened. Clearly I was failing at this enlightenment thing.

In my search for enlightenment, I've also spent weeks walking around telling myself over and over again that I am six feet tall and beautiful, but nary an inch showed on me (except maybe on my hips). I would close my eyes and sit listening to subliminals about how I was not my body and I could soar into the deepest realms of the universe, only to be woken up by my then three-year-old pounding on my face with her new plastic hammer toy, shouting "No sleep, Mama, no sleep!" That's right, honey bear, I am a no-sleep mama. And nope, no endless universe there. Somehow I couldn't make the connection between living my everyday life and ascending into the stars. There was a huge disconnect. Shocking, I know.

Today, the word or idea of enlightenment has more meanings than a porcupine has quills. After every seminar on the subject I attended, every book I read, every type of meditation and practice I attempted, the concept still eluded me. *Why?* I asked myself. *Why can't I be enlightened like everyone else?*

We know what the word means, but do we actually really know what enlightenment is? Is enlightenment actually something we can achieve, and is it something we should be seeking?

After years of study and many fireside chats with friends and gurus, I have come to realize that the concept of enlightenment from every form of study shares a common thread woven into myth, just as the stories told from culture to culture have similar themes and characters.

Many interpretations of enlightenment speak of complete surrender, a letting go of attachments to all that you believe in, even love, because you should love everything. They speak of a closeness to God, a complete sense of peace, like watching that guru on the stage all blissed out and smiling all the time—until you see them lose it at the airport over their seating assignment.

Some people suggest Transcendental Meditation as a way to find enlightenment. Others say that living in a cave in the Himalayas is the only way to true enlightenment. They believe that giving up all connection to the world is the only way to truly find your way back to the light. The definitions of enlightenment run the gamut from realizing your true self to creating balance in your life, and all the way to suddenly, with a grand poof, ascendance from this plane on to the next plane of mastery. It seems every belief has its own path to enlightenment. Now we've just got to pick the right one.

So I began a quest to understand the true meaning of enlightenment, because if I was going to walk around blindfolded in a field for six hours looking to manifest it, I had better know what it was.

I suppose when one begins a quest they should start at the beginning, but even that's an arguable point over cups of kombucha with friends.*

The idea of enlightenment is as old as the hills, and many ancient philosophies and practices talk of enlightenment, although they used different terms. Enlightenment became the word of the day because of its resemblance to the word *Bodhi* and the German word *Aufklarung*, used by philosopher Immanuel Kant in his 1784 essay *Answering the Question: What is Enlightenment?* Kant said, "Enlightenment is man's emergence from his self-incurred immaturity."[1] Which pretty much falls in line with what the Buddhists and Hindus meant when they used the words *Bodhi*, *kenshō*, and *satori*—all basically meaning to have woken up and understood, or to know one's true self. Basically, to be enlightened means we finally grew up!

In Buddhism (and I use that term loosely as there are multiple versions of Buddhism with different ideas about reaching enlightenment: so many roads, so many tunnels, so very confusing—sheesh), the idea is that one attempts to reach nirvana, Buddhahood (or enlightenment). Reaching Buddhahood means a full awakening and liberation from the attachments of our reality, instead of simply having insight into and certainty about it, or understanding it, which is a very Western idea of enlightenment. It's more than that. It's the big ah-ha! moment. It's being free once and for all from all the people, places, things, times, and events that have kept us chained in the prison of our suffering (and, in case you did not know it, we are all suffering).

Reaching this state of being takes years of practice and commitment and ultimately a total annihilation of self. Wow, that's quite the undertaking, and for me, something that seems utterly impossible. I mean it sounds great in theory, but who has time for total annihilation of self *and* grocery shopping? Because if that is what reality is about. How does a person truly seek enlightenment and live at the same time?

In the West, the idea of enlightenment has taken on a very romantic and, quite frankly, self-serving notion. There's something twisted about that. For millennia, enlightenment existed in the East as a noble, selfless goal; a few centuries in the West, and we've turned it into a romance story involving ourselves.

For most Westerners, the idea of enlightenment isn't about reaching total annihilation of ourselves and thus relieving ourselves of our attachments, ending the cycle of reincarnation, and moving onward into the next realm. As a Westerner (and if you were born in a Western country, you're pretty much stuck being one), I've got to say that that seems a lot to ask for. I doubt most us are really willing to give up all of our attachments, and I wonder if we should.

Enlightenment in the Western sense is really about gaining an insight into our true nature, an expression of a transcendent truth about who we are, a transcendental state of total acceptance and connectedness beyond the reach of any expressed language. Basically, it's an indescribable feeling of overwhelming love and connection to ourselves and everything known or unknown.

So, there is enlightenment (total annihilation of self) that means that you (I) have to be willing to let go of everything.[†] Then there is the kind of enlightenment reached through an understanding of self. If the choice is between annihilating it or understanding it, I think I'm going with understanding it. That's attainable. That's something I think I can eventually do. No annihilation needed here, thank you very much.

Many people speak of moments in their life when they have felt enlightened, when they had that ah-ha! moment. It's called an enlightened experience. I can remember moments in my life when everything felt so perfect, so connected that I couldn't even remember whether or not I existed. I was eternal. Moments when I experienced the totality of everything.

I remember once going camping and looking up into the night sky. I was in love, life was good, and the stars shone brighter than I'd ever seen them as they cruised the Milky Way. I didn't know if it was because I had a hot guy with me, a great glass of wine in me, or it was just one of those moments where everything felt right. Even the unknown didn't matter. But later, on the way home as I hit the smog-ridden freeway, the feeling was gone, and boy, did I want it again.

Like any good drug, once a moment of enlightenment happens, we begin to attempt to re-create that experience, and with every attempt it seems to get further and further away. Thus the eternal hunt through the maze for the cheese. The seeking becomes the endgame, and when we are seeking, we aren't really being.

Enlightenment isn't just associated with letting go of self or gaining knowledge of self—it is also associated with getting connected to our inner awesome; i.e., our divinity or our connection to it, depending on which belief path we are traveling. We see this in most ancient philosophies (yet another common thread) where the idea that we are divine beings full of love and light and everything that is "good" is a principal premise. It is said that divineness is already within us. So if we already have it, why, then, are we seeking it? It's truly a redundant question like, *Do you have DNA in your genetic material?* Erm, yes?

When I ask some of my favorite great minds about the idea of seeking enlightenment, they often say the same thing. My favorite is Austin Vickers, who told me, "Seeking enlightenment is like having a carrot on a string in front of you. It's attached to your head, but you think it's in front of you. Why would you seek something you already have? You've already experienced the whole love and light thing. You came here to experience the opposite, so that you could then appreciate the experience of fully loving, fully being in joy, even when it sucks." Okay, I added the word *sucks*. Austin wouldn't say sucks, but that's what he meant.

Maybe living with my feet firmly planted on the ground is divineness in action. A perfect example: Buddha. It's not like everything in Buddha's life was all lotus flowers and green tea. Sometimes he felt pain and sadness. And man, did he fully feel it. He held still and allowed himself to be present in that moment, and in that space he was able to understand how joyful, how awesome it is that we can experience the full extent of the emotions of an experience. He understood how amazing it is to be alive and to know both joy and sadness, to have loved so deeply that the loss of it hurts. He also knew that love is both constant and impermanent. Enlightenment isn't something we strive for; it is something felt in the moment. It's really just perspective. Can I see every experience in my life, even when it sucks, as a gift? Maybe not right then and there. Right then and there, I allow myself to feel angry, hurt, or embarrassed; later, after I've had time to gain perspective, I can see it as a gift.

The original concept of enlightenment, when splayed out for us to really see, requires us to be willing to let go of everything in our lives and see that it has no impact one way or another. But that's not me. Sometimes I cry, and sometimes I yell, and often I flail. That is me. Why annihilate the self when the self is what we have been given? There is a reason the cheese is so stinky. It wants to be experienced, felt in every corner of our olfactory glands. I mean, why have the sense of smell if we aren't going to use it?

That's what I've come to realize. I became addicted to the seeking. I became so desperate for that hunk of cheese that I forgot to look at the walls of the hallway, to enjoy the art, to see out the windows (that were even windows!). I needed to read that newest book, or the old one. I needed to make sure I had all the data so when enlightenment struck, I would know. I kept telling myself I didn't have it and I needed to get it.

So I've let go of seeking enlightenment. I've let go of judging myself for not being spiritual enough, for allowing myself to feel the way I feel and to experience life. When people ask if I'm on the path to enlightenment, I respond, how could I not be? Aren't we all? Unless, of course, you're asking if I'm attempting to kill off parts of me, the gifts I've been given to experience this life—then no. I'll keep those. I like them; they keep things interesting.

I've replaced my quest for enlightenment with acceptance of my life where it is, even happiness about where it is. I know—it's hard to be happy when things aren't going the way I want, when life is hard and I face struggle. Acceptance doesn't mean I've given up. You'll find I say that a lot in this book. I often have to remind myself of it. Struggle is part of life, and if we got everything we wanted all the time, we wouldn't be able to gain any wisdom, to shed any light of understanding about ourselves.

Ultimately, I believe that is what Buddha and all the other spiritual teachers meant when they spoke of enlightenment. Nirvana is when you know yourself. You know peace and connectedness both when it's easy and when it's hard. It takes practice and patience and love and forgiveness. Don't worry if you don't master it in a year or two. For most people, it takes at least one lifetime and probably more.

Now that's pretty enlightened, if I do say so myself.

Notes

* Info dump! Rumor has it that kombucha supposedly originated in China where it was said to have magical powers to help a person impressively live forever. It made its way to Russia and then the West, bringing with it the awesome reputation of being the best detoxifier of the body and mind in the *world* (according to its marketing and PR team). Currently, kombucha can be found being carried around in large glass mason jars by those recovering from all-night dance parties out in the woods along the Oregon coast.

† Oh, and I do mean everything: the car, the boyfriend, the kids and the dog, the ego, the knowing, the being right or even the being wrong, and the best parking spot. We have to be willing to awaken to a space in which none of that exists and it all exists simultaneously and where ultimately we don't really notice or care because we are simply just being, or maybe we cease being at all. Maybe we actually do go poof! I'd like to add some sparkles to that if it really is how it happens. Sparkles would add pizzazz.

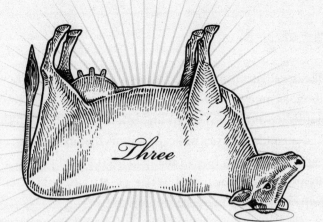

The Wacky Tale of Quantum Physics and Angel Cards and How It All Means Absolutely Nothing and Everything

So you're at a dinner party, and a really handsome guy is sitting across from you. He's charming, smart, and super cute. You've been digging deep in your How to Get That Hot Guy in Bed Handbook, and you've used just about everything it's got and still nothing. Suddenly you remember—because you learned it in this book—that when all else fails, if you use your sexiest voice (pull out your reading glasses if you have them or borrow someone's if you don't) and lay some of your cerebrally sexy quantum physics jargon on him, he'll quiver to attention like a well-strummed string theory. Chances are, he knows just about as much about it as you do, and that basically amounts to nothing. And I don't mean that ironically (mostly) in the sense that quantum physics basically tells us that matter is made up of basically nothing. I mean that you don't actually know anything about it. Who does, really? The point is that it's scientifically proven that guys like a sexy librarian.*

The only people who really understand the weird world of quantum physics are probably physicists, and even they will tell you they don't really understand much. This is not surprising. Quantum physics in action shows that reality—the world, the universe, and everything in it (or seemingly not in it)—is a very wacky place, filled with everything and nothing. It's a place where electrons can be in two of different places *simultaneously* (the quantum superposition principle goes one step further and theorizes that an electron can be all the possibilities of its self all at once), where an electron that bumped into another electron a billion years ago instantly knows what that other electron is doing even if it's a zillion light years away (entanglement). What quantum physics *is*, is science attempting to explain the nature of reality. What quantum physics is *not* is a religion, life philosophy, or a reason to stop taking your meds.

❚   ❚   ❚

Before we continue, let us review—quantum physics explained à la Betsy. Quantum physics is basically all about how the tiniest particles, so small that mitochondria have to use a microscope to see them, act upon and shape reality. The generally accepted take is that reality (material reality, the universe, everything and anything, the quantum foam† if you will), in terms of what quantum physics says about it, is an ever-shifting field of energy that is constantly reacting to "input." Input can mean anything from changing physical conditions in the universe to our individual thoughts and actions impacting the quantum field. As it turns out, even scientific measurement during experiments affects particles, determining their action (some like to say that is us affecting the measurement; some scientists don't like that assertion at all!). But if you're in the "we are doing it!" club, then basically quantum physics says that the stuff that makes up all of the stuff in the universe collapses into a finite particle when we pay attention to it or observe it. Until then, it's just a wave of possibility. I am still trying to make this happen with my hips when I "observe" them in the mirror and attempt to invoke the force to reduce them in size, but for whatever reason, my hips don't seem to want to play the quantum mash-up game. They are clearly only interested in reacting to another kind of input (chocolate, no doubt).

The take away, which is a doozy, is that our thoughts actually shape reality, at least a little bit. Of course, I don't know one person who has been able to shift reality from, say, a Honda to a Porsche without doing some serious heavy lifting of material stuff. Never mind that quantum physics says you're not actually touching material stuff, just energy. Oh, quantum physics, how you love to complicate things. And who needs any more complications in their life?

When I asked my favorite quantum physicist, Amit Goswami, PhD,‡ why I should care about understanding quantum physics, he promptly said, "The truth is, you probably shouldn't."

I took that to mean that knowing and caring about quantumisms is not going to get me anywhere near the reality of my life and the stuff that is important in it, like, you know, happiness—unless, of course, that guy across the table has a soft spot for a nerdy chick who can eloquently explain the distinction between the Heisenberg Uncertainty Principle and Schrödinger's Wave Equation (just for the record, I can, and for the record it hasn't gotten me laid, but I say, try and try again—even if it's a trick question).

▮ ▮ ▮

After years of hanging out with some pretty cool scientists as they tried to figure out the reality of our reality, it has become obvious to me that once we think we know something about anything quantum and come up with an awesome theory about it, the fucker is apt to change and shift. Next thing you know, a new understanding is riding in on a wave like we should have been expecting it all along. As a result, the one take away I have from understanding anything from quantum physics, which I will now share with you because I am kind and loving, dammit, is this: being willing to live in the mystery is something to really strive for. The blurrily known mystery can help you find the happiness you seek, grasshopper.

For the last decade or so, quantum physics has been all the New Age rage, and to be fair, I am guilty of perpetuating that tale—that super cute story of how Quantum met Perception, but then Attraction came on the scene and made an awkward love triangle, because Quantum could never stay true to either one for very long. That is to say, I made a film about how under-standing the wacky world of quantum was the answer to all our woes. And suddenly it became a religion, to some at least.

The movie spread the message, spawning an entire industry of quantum this and quantum that. I often imagine the infomercial dude—you know, the loud one, standing in front of the rows of people sitting with that awesome deer-in-headlights look as he presents the problem, only distorting the reality a tiny, big bit: did you know that if you truly understood the magnitude of the implications of quantum physics on reality, you would simply vanish off the face of the earth? It's that wacky! But don't worry, folks (phew—audience wipes collective brow)! Understanding quantum reality also means that you will ascend immediately into the realms of the gods! You will be able to hang out with Fred Alan Wolfe (also known as Dr. Quantum) and party like a Higgs boson, out of sight, but totally there to make your quantum ride the best it can be!

"Everything we call real is made of things that cannot be regarded as real. If quantum mechanics hasn't profoundly shocked you, you haven't understood it yet." So says Niels Bohr.[§]

So, Niels, what I'd really like to know is, what exactly am I supposed to do with that? Hmm, no answer. I mean it's cool, really cool, but this is a book about finding happiness, not the Higgs boson. And sometimes I worry that we get caught up in "knowing" cool stuff for the sake of knowing it, and we lose what really matters.

Okay, I'm here to cause some quantum discord. This isn't going to be a place where I regale in the mystical magical world of quantum physics, turning old Niels into a quantum God; this is where I'm going to nucleate that myth like a good old can of Coke and Mentos explosion. Well, sort of (okay, just for clarification, the term quantum discord doesn't really mean discord; it actually means finding a correlation between two nonclassical [entangled/joined] subsystems—so in fact, it's actually correlated, not uncorrelated, but only in the nonclassical sense. Now go look that up and let me get to my point). It sounded good so I went with it, and I bet if I hadn't said anything you would have simply nodded your head and laughed. That's what I usually do, so just go with me here. My point is, understanding quantum physics is essentially not going to really do anything for you. It has absolutely no bearing on whether or not you're going to be happy or enlightened. It's not going to win you the lottery or get you laid. Your ability to describe the nature of reality in terms of bosons, electrons, and particles is not going to help you when your kid has just eaten a Sharpie and you're trying to figure out if his lips look cute in neon blue or if you should call poison control.

Understanding the Planck scale[ll] is not going to bring you inner peace and is more likely to exhaust you as you surf the ever-cresting waves of possibilities. And I know you've read *In Search of Schrödinger's Cat: Quantum Physics and Reality*,[1] and maybe it blew your mind, but are you finally happy and fulfilled and able to die knowing you've learned everything you've come here to learn about quantum physics? I'm going to bet no. You want to know where knowing about this stuff will really help with your life? If you are at a party going for the hot guy doing the sexy librarian thing, then understanding these things might help you get, erm, enlightened in a different way.

Knowing about the ins and outs of quantum stuff will also help you greatly in your life if you are, in fact, a physicist.

And, okay, I admit it, it is fun to explore the idea that we are forever riding a wave of possibility until we believe (observe) and that possibility becomes a reality (a particle). Plus, I enjoy whipping out my quantum chatter at a party when someone has me pegged for the dumb blonde. But, after mumble-mumble years of riding that wave, the truth is, it wasn't what brought me peace.

Why? Because ultimately, knowing about science isn't what brings peace and happiness. Okay, maybe it does if you're a scientist, or a science enthusiast, and it's your soul's desire to know science, but often it isn't the answer you're looking for. We like to use science to ground us, because we like proof. We like to be able to say, "Because science says so." It's sort of like saying "Because I said so" to your kids.

We really do like a good metaphor, and some of quantum physics can be used as a good metaphor for life. One of my favorites is the quantum leap. Quantum leaps may be across distances, but one example commonly spoken of in quantum physics occurs when an electron makes a jump from one energy level to another and does so without traveling through any of the points in between. No time passes in the leap and there is no gradual ramping up of the energy. Just presto, an electron goes from one quantum state to another!

When we hear that someone has made a quantum leap in life, we usually think that person has made some huge, seemingly instantaneous life change. We might even think of the old television show *Quantum Leap* and picture someone diving through a wormhole and instantly coming out the other side in a whole new reality replete with a new house, car, and wife. But while we use these words and images as metaphors to describe big changes, in physics a quantum leap is in fact a very, very, very small leap.

Here's another metaphor: Physics says that everything is mostly empty space, which could be taken to mean that nothing is really solid. It's cool to know that not because you can use that information to walk through the bathroom wall to get away from a really bad date, but to understand that appearances can be deceiving. What we see isn't always what we think we see (because usually we're thinking from our lazy brain and not our conscious one). So instead of trying to shape-shift in order to get away from that bad date, you should probably be asking yourself what you saw in that guy in the first place. My point is, even if science doesn't bring peace and happiness, it can be helpful to understand that some things we understand to be true scientifically can be used metaphorically.

To be fair to all us quantum enthusiasts, it appears that quantum physics is showing us that most things you think you know about yourself probably aren't true. You're more amazing than you could even imagine, and reality is probably far more mind boggling than you realize. More mind boggling than I can explain here. The universe is a truly an amazing thing (if it is a thing, which would assume that it's real—but I'm going stop right there and neatly sidestep that rabbit hole).

The reality is, and I hate to burst your particle, but it's highly unlikely you're going to be able to change anything in your reality with just a thought. In my humble opinion, the concept is simply mental masturbation. Yep, I just said that. It is a rabbit hole; it's not a religion or a life philosophy. While it may be fun to fall down the quantum wormhole for a mind-bending session with friends over dinner, and while it is useful in helping explain the nature of reality, it is not really great at solving our big, macro life problems.

I I I

This is one of my biggest sacred cows: the difference between talking about it and being it, philosophy (or intellectual mumbo jumbo) versus practical application. We humans love our cows whether they're in the form of quantum physics, crystals, aura readings, or (insert any of your favorite New Age fetishes or spiritual rituals here). We have a habit of making these things our dogma, our religion.* Instead of being open to all the possibilities of our own amazing abilities, we use things like quantum physics as a way to avoid looking at ourselves and the reality we're sitting in, right here and right now. In my opinion, the talismans we wear have simply become a way to escape from doing the real work on the big talismans we were born with—our intuition and our ability to reason things out and get beyond our emotional responses. We have become so desperate for the quick fix that we believe our talismans are really going to save our asses when the red and blue lights flash behind us, so we speed along in life, not actually realizing that we should probably just drive the speed limit. You and the cop may be one, but you're still going to get a ticket, and that shit is real and expensive. We expect that having an understanding of the workings of the universe will somehow give us the power to control it, but just like expecting the universe to divvy up the spoils (as in, asking the universe or God or anyone else for the stuff we want), once again we're giving our true power to anything but ourselves. It's time to take it back.

At the risk of alienating a lot of people who might "like" me on Facebook, none of that "stuff" really matters—not your birth sign, not the cycle of the moon, not the fact that Mercury is in retrograde for like the thousandth time this year. It wasn't until someone told me about the whole Mercury issue that it actually began to fuck with me (hmm, think about that for a minute).

There are many interesting studies in which people are given a placebo (fake) pill, surgery, or test. In these studies, the people who take the placebo sometimes have just as much success as the people taking the real deal. Sometimes they even have more, especially if the real deal isn't so great. The people who took the placebo didn't know that's what they were getting; they just believed it would have an effect. Sort of like when my computer and phone took a nosedive right after I heard from a friend how Mercury was messing with her life. Was it really Mercury wreaking havoc, or was it my own belief that it was Mercury—does it matter? I believed, and that's all it took. I observed it to be true, and it was. But is this really the observer effect in action? Or am I just seeing what I want to see? I guess it just depends on what you believe.

So here we are back at belief again. Wow, that little word is so powerful. For the record, I am not suggesting you throw out your dream catcher or tear up your animal cards. Go ahead and have your aura photographed and read that book on quantum physics. It is possible that seeing that dark circle around you in your aura photograph will finally force you to deal with the true issues, like why you keep dating the wrong men or taking jobs that make you feel miserable, or why you need an aura picture to tell you what you probably already instinctively know. Because we do usually already know what we need to know; we just have a tendency to ignore such things until something finally pushes us over the edge. If it's the flipping of the angel card, so be it.

But just remember, my dear, you are part of the quantum foam. Your electrons are made of the same stuff that makes up the universe and that angel card. If we are truly connected to everything (entangled) as they say, then ultimately, everything comes from you and me and your friends and that hot guy across the dinner table. Not the aura picture, the animal cards, or the crystal around your neck. Because we are indeed the dream weavers. We are the creatives, and everything comes from us, not the other way around.

Be careful not to let your ego go crazy here. I don't mean this in some narcissistic "it's all about me" way, although you could run with that if you want. It simply means that when your psychic tells you that you will meet the man of your dreams on a beach as you tumble out of the water, chances are you're going to book the first flight to Tahiti and spend days, waterlogged and pruney and with sand in places you didn't know existed, waiting for him. Because you believe with every ounce of your being everything your psychic tells you, it's probably going to happen, even if that guy ends up being a douche five years later. Why? Because you believed it and took action. Basically, unless you do something about it, that bunny foot isn't going to do it for you. You are the accelerant, you are the observer in your life, and everything starts and ends with you. So check in with yourself before you buy that ticket; ask yourself why you want that man and why it has to be Tahiti (although, if you're going to jump on a plane to meet a man, it might as well be in Tahiti).

One of the fun things quantum physics tells us is that there is a probability for everything. This is loosely based on the Copenhagen interpretation, which (in its boiled-down form) says that all of the possibilities available in the wave aspect of matter will immediately collapse into one "finite" particle-like event upon observation in an experiment. Hence the saying "collapsing into reality," which is very popular in the New Age community, mostly because it's nice to think we have the power to collapse reality. And in a way, we do, just probably not the way we'd like to think we do. If you want to bring the micro out into the macro, go from possibility to reality, then see it like this: your life is the experiment, and you are the observer, but it's not going to happen unless there is action on your part. Someone's got to drop the first particle into the cylinder. The questions you should be asking are, *What action am I taking?* and *From what place within me am I taking that action?*

All of these talismans are tools you can use. If it makes you feel better to know you have your lucky rabbit's foot, then carry it. If you want to check your horoscope before you make that important call, do it. If you want to understand the inner workings of "reality," read that quantum physics book. But don't give away your true power. The power in knowing that, really, everything you seek you have, if you observe it as so. Maybe not the car, but the wisdom to know how to get the car. Maybe not the guy, but the wisdom to know you didn't want him anyway.

It's all stored neatly within the amazing quantum computer you carry around with you all the time: you—your brain, your body, consciousness (which is either inside or outside of you depending on whom you ask; it's that piece of you science has yet to explain). Take a moment to think about what your brain and your body are doing right now. It's pretty amazing, isn't it? And if they can do that, imagine what else they're capable of doing. Who or what is the part of you that knows the answers before you ask the question? Who or what is the part of you that sees you in the world? What is *that you* capable of doing? Rabbit's foot or no rabbit's foot. You are, in fact, the quantum accelerator.

And here is another reason quantum physics is cool. Quantum physics says we are inextricably connected to each other and to everything because all matter is made of energy and it all hangs out in the quantum field or, you might say, The Void. If you want to have some conscious choice about how those waves end up as particles, you have to have awareness (be conscious) of those waves of potential. You have to be aware that things are the way they are because you are perceiving (observing) them that way, and if you want to change your reality, you have to be willing to change the way you see your reality. You have to be willing to hang out with your other self. In order to change the way you see your reality, it's important to know that other possibilities exist and then be willing to sit with the un-comfortableness of the unknown. We have to get quiet enough to hear the waves of possibilities, see the waves, feel the waves. We don't need anything else (shoot, and I just invested in a whole new set of angel cards), just the willingness to be; and once we've been for a while, we can make a choice to do. Amit Goswami calls it the "do be do be do."[2]

You can pick any way you want to do this being—meditate on a cushion, listen to music, do yoga, or exercise. I find that hanging out in my back yard, listening to the birds while I spend time trimming the roses, helps me find my being space. Me and the flowers just being one together. But sometimes it takes sitting with the conflict instead of shoving it aside in favor of smelling the roses. Holding the idea that many outcomes are possible—that's a piece of quantum that is useful to you right now. We're quick to want to resolve and make up, but being in the space you are in and holding the juxtaposition creates the opportunity for the new thought to arrive. Essentially, sometimes it's best to just hang out in the foam with all the other cool waves, patiently waiting until you see the one you really want to collapse. Without even realizing it, the answer to my contemplation floats on a wave into my consciousness; I observe it, and poof, it's a particle. But I caution you to be realistic in how you view your reality. There is nothing more embarrassing than leaving a store and telling the nice man carrying your heavy box to put it in the back of the Porsche while standing in front of a Kia, or attempting to create a grand exit and walking into a wall.

Notes

* There is proof! Or at least a discussion about how *sexy* and *librarian* coexist, simultaneously in the same person. There is this thesis, written in 2005 as part of an MA requirement for the University of Maryland, College Park.

The author, one Christine Ann Lutz, gave her thesis the rather awesome title of *From Old Maids to Action Heroes: Librarians and the Meanings of Librarian Stereotypes*. To learn about Lipstick Librarians and Librarian Avengers (who would have thought?) check it out at: http://drum.lib.umd .edu/bitstream/1903/2670/1/umi-umd-2587.pdf.

† Quantum foam is the term coined by John Wheeler as a way to get your head around the stuff that everything, all of the particles and fields and matter that are the universe, schmooze around in . . . the primordial ooze of the universe, if you would like a loose metaphor, in which everything does its thing, except instead of ooze you imagine it as foam. It is the roux of the universal stew, if you want another, even looser metaphor. Quantum foam can also be used as a way to say, "Time ain't smooth, it's a hot foamy mess." The concept is still a little frothy (har-har) as new experiments and data shed more light on how such a concept fully acts in and on space and time.

‡ If you don't have a favorite quantum physicist, I'm telling you, right here, that all the cool people have one—a favorite quantum physicist that is. I'm nerdy enough to say that it is outright fun to have conversations with someone who creates mathematical stories that look like art using symbols that look like a mix of Egyptian and Mayan hieroglyphs, and who talks about things like the God particle (officially it's called the Higgs boson, but God particle sounds sexier). Inner geek says "squee!"

§ If you are just checking into the quantum universe, Niels Bohr is pretty much one of the godfathers of modern quantum mechanics. He won a Nobel Prize in physics and, most coolly, helped Jews during World War II. Then, after a daring escape from Denmark, was one of the team that developed the nuclear bomb; the coolness factor on that one is conflicted.

|| Here's the Planck scale as explained by me, nerdy layperson. Named for Max Planck, it theorizes that there is a point when there are enough quantum particles at the party to start actually acting on gravity, and it becomes

comparable to all other fundamental forces. An implication of that nifty idea is of great interest in that the quantum possibilities, since they are now acting on gravity, can theoretically be said to exist in the relative world, the world that we see in our daily lives set in time and space. And because the observer effect, not to be confused with the Heisenberg Uncertainty Principle, shows that we can change how quantum particles act when we pay attention to them, it means that if we are impacting particles at the quantum level, and at that level there is a point when the particles gather enough magic mojo to act in the relative universe, then we can, by force of consistent observation, actually shift the world around us on different levels. The truth is (as I've been told by many a physicist—most recently Dean Radin) that it takes practice for an observer to really make anything bigger than a particle do anything worth measuring. In other words, I guess staring for hours at my Kia and attempting to will it into a Porche is not going to work.

\# If you were looking for a very dry but descriptive explanation of the connection between quantum physics and spirituality, you might read this. If you can get through it, call me and we'll hang out: http://www.theistic science.org/talks/qps1/.

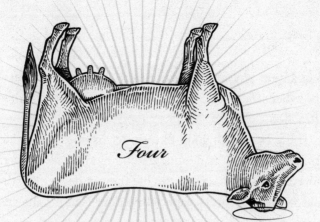

What the Hell Is the
Law of Attraction Anyway?

As long as we're on the subject of sacred cows of the New Age world, besides quantum physics, crystals, and dolphin pendants, there are a couple of other big bovines I'd like to tip over: "the Law of Attraction" and "I create my reality." These catchy idioms were made famous by two films that broke out into the mainstream back in the early 2000s and spawned an entire industry around their concepts. Of course, I'm partial to *What The Bleep Do We Know!?* because I was one of the filmmakers. This film popularized the notion through comparisons to quantum physics that we, in fact, literally create our reality. The other, *The Secret*, told us that like attracts like—the Law of Attraction.

These were both good films in terms of exposing ideas and concepts that, if truly understood and used properly, can indeed help people create the life they so desire. But they may have in some respects, especially in our "tell me the answer in thirty seconds" generation, done more harm than good, because these concepts are intricate and hard to completely explore in a ninety-minute film. I'm sure I won't do them justice in just one chapter. These two ideas have a lot of similarities in their meanings, including the fact that both hinge on the idea that what you think, you get. Both are great concepts, but each has its own set of pitfalls.

So what is the Law of Attraction? This concept basically states that like attracts like, and in terms of quantum physics, it says that like energy attracts like energy. So if your energy is no bueno, then you're going to get no bueno. We first heard this with the *Think and Grow Rich* books, which in my humble opinion did a good job of explaining that it's more than just an attitude or a thought: there is a work ethic involved in your thinking and doing. Esther and Jerry Hicks brought it home with the book *The Law of Attraction*, and it became all the rage with *The Secret*, which has made the concept a little too simplistic for my taste (now, now, I'll take *Bleep* to task in a minute).

I seem to have been born with a good attitude and pretty positive outlook. I know, I know. So far it seems like all I've been telling you about is the supposed bad stuff, like how I hated my body and my life fell apart and I got divorced. But through every crisis in my life, I have always had the ability to pick myself up, dust myself off, and as the Brits say, carry on (maybe not always calmly, but carry on I have). So when I first heard this idea of like attracts like, it made perfect sense to me, and I was pretty good at it. Some would even say I was an idiot savant.

My life has had many incarnations—actress, filmmaker, gourmet dog treat entrepreneur (yeah, that's a non sequitur). With each incarnation I carried some sort of innate belief that I would succeed, at least at the beginning. And I did. I owned my own production company by the age of twenty-two, I was a senior executive at a production company by the time I was twenty-five (as a chick, no less!), and believe it or not, at one point my dog treats could be found in almost four hundred stores across the country. But for some reason, this ability to succeed would evaporate into a fear that somehow I wasn't worthy of success and boom, out would fall the bottom. As a child actress I did more than a hundred commercials, appeared on popular TV shows, and did a few movies, which will remain nameless. Somewhere later in my career (at the ripe old age of fifteen) the doubt and fears began to take hold and success began to elude me. It became harder and harder to get what I wanted, no matter how much I "believed" in myself. With each role I did not get, I began to take on the belief that maybe I wasn't all that. Inwardly the insecurity began to fester, even though outwardly I was still pretty optimistic. I wasn't prepared to deal with my insecurities. They contradicted my outward belief that I was all that, so I hid them in the shadows and could not understand why I wasn't achieving all the goals I had set for myself. This pattern followed me for my entire life. Easy success in the beginning followed by a very long, and yet oddly swift, fall to the bottom.

It's easy to believe in the dream in the beginning when it's still fresh. To set our intentions and go after it with all the gung ho of Alfalfa, Buckwheat, and Spanky getting ready to put on a show. But the trick with this whole Law of Attraction thing is that it doesn't really pay attention to the layer of "I can do it" you've smeared over the doubt and fear of failure that's hidden underneath. It's really answering that true self, the one we're most likely pretending doesn't exist.

The Law of Attraction isn't something you employ at will. It doesn't appear at the clap of your hands like your personal court jester to amuse you and deliver what you desire. It's really on autopilot, always in action, but it's you who needs to actually do the work from the inside out, not the other way around.

And no, vision boards are not the work of which I speak, though yes, vision boards are fun and give us something to do on New Year's Eve instead of drinking ourselves into oblivion, hoping to drown out the dread of yet another year of the same old misery. They give us hope, and that's a good thing. But hope doesn't put food on the table, and it doesn't buy those Christian Louboutins you've been eyeing at Nordie's. Hope is great, but it won't bring you true happiness or peace. Hope without action is like staring at a weight-loss inspired vision board every day while eating a box of glazed donuts.

One of the interesting things often said about the Law of Attraction is the idea that you are supposed to act like you already have it, that you are it, and say the all-powerful "I am (insert whatever it is you want to be here)." I can sit for hours visualizing my life on my own private island, with my perfect children playing in the surf and my gorgeous husband Ryan Gosling rubbing suntan lotion on my back. But somehow Ryan just hasn't shown up yet. I can absolutely fake it until I make it, uttering "I am Mrs. Ryan Gosling, I am Mrs. Ryan Gosling, I am Mrs. Ryan Gosling" like I have Tourette's, but therein lies the downfall of the whole concept. Faking it isn't actually being it, and the longer you fake it, the deeper you're going to bury the truth about what you really believe. Unless while you're faking it to the world, you're also doing the inside work of uncovering why you need to fake it in the first place. Because telling yourself something over and over again when you truly do not believe it with every inch of your being is akin to trying to convince the tax man that chocolate is a write-off because it was research for your next book about what makes people happy. It may sound good when you say it, but that doesn't make it a reality. We can trick even particles for a little while, but eventually that Law of Attraction catches on and figures out we're full of shit.

For more than forty years I perfected the calm, cool, and collected face. The one with the smile that radiates a warm and compassionate being—come on, you know the type. I exuded success while underneath I truly felt, well, like shit. And with each new dream, I hid that belief so well that it took a while for this Law of Attraction thingamajig to figure it out—I can be crafty, you know. Hence why I was initially successful and then suddenly not.

Way back in 2001, after my gourmet dog treat company had basically burned up like an overcooked chicken cookie,

I stumbled upon the notion that maybe I wasn't actually living my dream, my soul's desire. Without realizing it, I began to do the work necessary to get what I truly wanted. After I had dumped my gig as a cool Hollywood-producing It Girl and burned my dog treat business over a broken heart, my car had been repossessed and I had pretty much lost all my friends, save a few. Clearly my life was a hot mess, and it didn't take a quantum physicist to figure that out. All my knowledge of quantum would come later, and my life would still end up a hot mess (which is why understanding quantum does not equal happiness).

Before I made *Bleep* and went all New Age on myself, one of my friends convinced me to go to a yoga class with her. Which was sort of a joke—we've all heard the stories about first yoga experiences and mine was no different. But I went. I rode my red bike across town and entered a big room filled with sinu-ous-looking women who aggravated my "I'm short and fat" insecurity. I lumbered through the class until finally it was time to meditate, which for me meant take a nap. The teacher appeared above my head (even though my eyes were closed, I could tell because her voice boomed over me), and as if she was speaking directly to me, she said something to the effect of, "Your life is a mess because you're not being clear about what you want. Go figure it out. Make a list." Okay, I paraphrased that. When she basically told me to get my shit together, she was way more eloquent with her lilting voice and the words breathed out in that measured way only a yoga teacher can do. I swear they have to pass a class in the melodic hum of yoga in order to be certified.

As I rode home, I contemplated what she had said. It was the first time I had ever heard of a yoga instructor saying anything remotely close to "make a list." Meditate, yes. An orderly column of orderly thoughts, not so much.

Meditating had never made sense to me. I'm a ball of nervous energy, and sitting still is just not something I do well, but a list of what I wanted in life, I could make. This was obviously the precursor to the vision board—we've become so crafty in this new millennium. The list, as a way to figure your shit out, is a throwback tool used in basically every century before this one.

So I went home and made my list. But for some reason, instead of rushing to write down whatever randomly popped into my head (my usual modus operandi), I actually thought about it. I lit a candle and seriously spent time with my thoughts. This was new! My thoughts usually freaked me out so I didn't like hanging out with them, but I forced myself to really examine them. I knew that this was important, even without understanding how I knew it was important. I felt as if writing this would either save my life or kill me. It was do or die, and I could feel it with every ounce of my being. I knew I wanted to find my life, my happiness, and this was going to lead me there. Looking back on that time now, I know the voice that sat me down that day was my inner voice, my intuition. She and I have become friends since then.

I took my time gathering my materials. I found my favorite magnolia-scented candle, the big fat one that I knew would last for hours, days if I needed it to, and I borrowed my dog's bed so I could sit on the floor and not have to hunch over. I wanted to be as comfortable as possible. I made sure I had plenty of smokes and Cokes to get me through so I wouldn't have to leave if I didn't need to. I hunkered down and I began to write out my life using my favorite pen and a brand-new, never-been-cracked-open journal bought with the last few dollars I had to my name.

On the first day I wrote about everything wrong in my life—my career, my love life, money, friends. I thought about all the times in my life I had been hurt and the times I had hurt others. I spent several days in negativity land, in fact, angry at myself, angry at the people in my life then and the ones I had kicked out. I cried and was truly depressed. About five days in, I looked down at my beautiful new journal and all I saw was darkness and misery. Then that new voice that I was just getting to know reminded me, "You're supposed to be writing what you want, not what you don't want." Duh! No wonder I felt like shit. So I ripped out all the dark pages, and although my journal wasn't as pristine as it had been, I started anew. My trusty pen waiting, my candle burning, I waited and listened for the right questions to come, and when they did, the answers flowed out as if they had been there all along.

I asked myself what I truly loved, and I answered making films. But I didn't want to make just any film. I wanted to make films that spoke to people's hearts and that gave them hope and inspired them. I asked myself where I wanted to live, and I answered that I was tired of LA and wanted to move to a new place, something I had never done. I asked myself what kind of love I wanted, and I answered passionate, all-encompassing love. I asked myself what was my biggest fear at the moment, and I answered the debt I carried after the failure of my business. It took me thirty days to come to these answers. It took courage to face what my life had been and how I'd gotten to where I was. It took honesty to be real about who I had been and who I wanted to become, and it took belief in myself and the belief that what I truly desired, I could achieve. But the amazing thing was that I had never read a book about quantum physics or the Law of Attraction. I hadn't meditated a minute in my life, and I had no idea what I was doing, but I believed with all my being I needed to do it and that I could.

You could call it beginner's luck, but sometimes I think ignorance is bliss because within sixty days of writing that list, I had everything on it. I had been hired to make *Bleep*, I had moved to Washington, I had met my (now ex-)husband, and I was out of debt.

And then I got cocky. I decided this manifesting thing, this Law of Attraction trick, was easy, and I didn't have to work at it anymore. It took ten years for me to build that castle and about three minutes to tear it down. Well, the truth is, I was tearing it down as I was building it, because I was using shoddy building materials, not fully developed understandings. But I either didn't see that I was missing the point, or I shoved it deep into the bowels of my dungeon of doubt, because ten years later everything I had "manifested" was gone. My marriage to my "soul mate" was over, *Bleep* was still there but almost a distant memory, and I was back in LA and broke. Only now I was a single mom with no real way to earn a living, and no idea what I wanted to do or what I could do. I was just in pure survival mode.

I was shocked and surprised to find myself back where I had started almost ten years earlier, sitting on my floor with a burning candle and making yet another list. I was angry for a while. I didn't want to hear from one more person how everything has a purpose or that I should meditate. No amount of knowledge about the workings of the universe could fix this, and the Law of Attraction was bullshit because I certainly did not attract this! I was the *Bleep* girl, for fuck sake. I am the amazing manifester of all things wonderful. This shit does not happen to me!

When we suffer a loss, we go through many stages of grief, and I was hunkered down in denial. But there was one thing I couldn't do, no matter how hard I tried. I couldn't undo what I knew—that the only way I was going to get my life together was to start over and make a new list. It had actually worked the first time, and I had gotten everything on it that I asked for. When I made that list, I had found my inner voice, and she helped me believe I was worthy of my dreams. I had just lost her somewhere along the way. By finding that inner voice, I had peeled back one layer of my onion, and it worked for a while. Now I needed the willingness to dig deeper into myself to weed out the stubborn roots of my past. I guess the old saying "if at first you don't succeed, try, try again" makes sense here. Although now I understand that it wasn't a failure; it's a process.

What I learned about the Law of Attraction was that it wasn't a gimmick or a toy I could whip out at parties. It was real, but not in the way I had understood it. The Law of Attraction works because it gives you exactly what you are being—like attracts like—no bullshit, no floating on the bubbles of bliss, and no riding the quantum foam. You can fake it all you want, but unless you dig up the bones of your beliefs and make the necessary changes, you will only get what you are really asking for. You will only get what you're truly emanating into the quantum field. No matter how many nice thoughts and vision boards you have, no matter what you're asking for, if there are a bunch of defeatist, victim, angry, lack-filled subconscious programs floating around in your brain, *that's* what you get. So be careful what you ask for, and be clear in what you ask for. And be patient with yourself, because getting what you really want sometimes takes getting what you don't want first. And sometimes (most of the time), what you get is probably what you need in order to finally understand what to ask for.

That other ginormous adage we love to shout out for all to hear, as if we really want to lay claim to it, is "I create my reality!" Okay, I'm guilty of perpetuating this baby. To be fair to both films (*The Secret* and *Bleep*), we did have good intentions, and we weren't completely off base.

But guess what. You don't really create your reality. Some say reality is collectively created through our collective consciousness (since we're all connected). Others say it was created by accident, and still others say a big guy in the sky built it as his ultimate playground and torture chamber. And yes, it is made up of all sorts of cool things like electrons, quarks, and other particles, but again, all that is just mental masturbation. If anyone tells you they know, emphatically and without a doubt, what reality is, then they are either the second coming of Jesus or an arrogant asshole who needs to go read another book (and since I like to think I'd recognize the second coming of Jesus if I were, you know, there when it happened, my money's on the "go read another book" option).

Even if the observer affects reality, mostly we only do it on a very, very (insert very-infinity here) small level, and individually you aren't really creating the reality of the chair you're sitting in to read this book. Okay, maybe you went to a store and bought it, but magically manifesting it out of thin air—I think not. It's probably still there even when you're not. I believe that what you're really creating is your opinion of reality, your experience of it, which, as I have said, is tainted by your beliefs about it. In other words, while it's true that when you step in that pile of dog poo in your yard, you can perceive it any way you like and therefore create a reality in which you see that pile of poo as a gift to your grass or as a nuisance, but you still have to figure out how to get it out of the nifty grooves in your tennis shoes. And thus the mundaneness of life rains on your reality parade just a little bit, and you are left feeling vaguely damp. Then, in your newly dampened state, you begin to ask questions like "Why on earth did I bring this dog poo into my life?" and "What's my lesson here?" because we New Agers love to see the meaning in everything, even the dog poo, and we love nothing more than an existential quest into the meaning of said dog poo.

Can't it just be poo? Must I find some kind of awesome meaning in scraping the shit out of my shoe grooves? I mean, I *can*, but *should* I? Because here's the real deal—at least the way I've decided to perceive it. You did not reach into the quantum field and manifest that poo in order to send yourself a message of deep meaning. The dog simply pooped. It's neutral poop.

The same pretty much goes for car accidents, ski accidents, and even the fun stuff like when you see signs for Hawaii everywhere and you begin to think, "I need to go to Hawaii." Can't it just be that Hawaii is on a big advertising kick? While it may be true that you need a vacation, the universe probably isn't sending you messages about it. The universe is neutral until you make it your own reality; the meaning is coming from you, not the other way around. You will see what you want to see and attach the meaning that best suits what you think you want, so if you've been hankering for a trip to Hawaii, well, you're going to find a way to get there. But it's still your hankering.

I jumped on the "I create my reality" bandwagon pretty quickly, and why wouldn't I? At the time, my life was going pretty damn great, so of course I wanted to take credit for it, but that meant I also had to take credit for the times in my life when it wasn't all peachy keen. I had to take credit for both the shit and the roses. Again, because my life was pretty good at the time of this "I create my reality" realization, I must have felt I needed all that stink in order to smell the roses.

But here's the thing about "creating reality." When we choose to attach meaning to something, the meaning we're most likely to attach is the one that comes out of the belief machine in our head. So yes, you are indeed "creating a reality," but (and I'll say this again, because it bears repeating) instead of thinking you magically dropped that chunk of reality there, you should be wondering *why* you are attaching the meaning you are attaching to the collections of particles in front of you. How do you want to see that long line of traffic in the morning? Is it an opportunity to listen to that awesome book, or is it a hindrance because you're late, or is it just traffic? How you perceive things and how you respond are what create your reality. Reality is just reality, and I've decided I have enough meaning in my life, and a little discernment is a good thing. There is a time and a place for meaning, and it's not always in the dog poo.

I hope you're relieved now that you can let go of finding meaning in why your dog loves to poop in your favorite part of the garden. But even if not everything has to have a meaning, it's also possible that everything could be an opportunity to fine-tune your behavior and learn a thing or two about yourself in order to not have to constantly search for meaning.

A good place for this kind of nuanced fine-tuning of behavior, for me anyway, is in the relationships with the people we surround ourselves with. It can be fun (or traumatizing, depending on the relationship) to *really* look at how you behave and how you react to another person (the meanings you attach to them and their actions). Your behavior and your reaction (not theirs) can tell you a lot about yourself. The spiritual premise that is often used in conjunction with this is that the people in your life are mirrors for you to reflect upon your own self. You "attract" them because you need to learn something about yourself or maybe you need to learn something from the encounter. I believe that this is true to some extent, because we can learn from how we interact with other people. But are you really manifesting these people in order to learn something, or are you simply responding to the beliefs you already have about yourself and gravitating toward the people who agree with your beliefs? Or is it the same thing?

Here's a fun word: responsibility. If I am the creator of my own reality, then I am creating/attracting everyone in it. Wow, that's a lot of responsibility. Suddenly I am not only responsible for me, but also for them and everything they do, because somehow it's all because of me. Can you spell narcissistic?

▌   ▌   ▌

In my relationships, it took me a while to realize that I am the one doing the doing because the lens through which I participate in the world is mine. This was a relief, this realization, because if I was doing the doing in my life, that meant everyone else was doing the doing in their lives. Suddenly I was able to let go of the idea that I could or should do the doing for anyone else, that it was, in fact, impossible to be accountable for creating or maintaining someone else's reality and decisions. I can self-determine exactly one person, and that person is me. What's important is my ability to respond.

Which led me to finally understand that I am responsible for me, my reactions, and my responses to input from others. The people in my life are not doing anything to me in order for me to "learn." They are simply being themselves, and I am attaching meaning to their behaviors based on my beliefs. Furthermore, I realized that if I took a moment to really listen and pay attention, instead of simply slapping my beliefs like a voiceover on top of their pretty faces, I would realize that a lot of interactions probably aren't going to go where I truly want them to go.

I will say that I have had my not so great moments when I got really honest with myself and acknowledged that I had, indeed, *invited* people into my life who, from my end of things, sucked. It is a hard thing to say, it was *me*. *I* had that drink, *I* went home with him, and *I* married a couple of the "hims." Okay, for full disclosure, I have been married twice, once when I was very young and even more confused than the second time.

But no one operates in a vacuum, and sometimes you have to stop yourself and realize that the people in your life are doing their own doing in the same life-scenes that you are a part of. Like actors in a play, we all feed off the energy and the nuance of one another to create the stories of our lives, both the joint story and the singular story. And that is how and why we mutually feed into, on, and off the set beliefs we have established about ourselves. We're hearing our set of beliefs, and they are hearing theirs, and neither of us is really listening. When you realize that, your behavior around people will change.

And there it is. Another reality that is mundane but highly significant: we change throughout our lives. And we don't change at the same pace as one another. Which means that sometimes, when we change our beliefs and the other person is still feeding off the way it was, we may find that the other person sort of doesn't belong there anymore. When that happens, it's necessary to collect what we can from them and move on. In the process of doing this, you might find a silver bullet of understanding about yourself and why this person was in your life in the first place. Learning this about yourself may be hard, but you will if you're willing to be honest.

But then what? Once you've had this ah-ha! moment, and you've uncovered some belief about yourself, this person doesn't just suddenly evaporate or melt away. I know, I know. "They" say the people who no longer match your energy go away. Unfortunately, that's not always how it goes. Sometimes you're stuck with them, in which case you have to change your reality about them.

This was the case with my divorce. I have kids with my ex-husband, and he's not going anywhere anytime soon, even though I have changed and I "believe" he hasn't, at least not in the way I expected him to (expectations are a real doozy). I stood around for a long time waiting for him to change, thinking that since I created my reality, I had also created him in order to learn what I needed to learn. I felt like I had learned all that I could from him, so why wasn't he doing the dance my puppeteer hands were demanding he do? What did I do to create this? Why wasn't he doing what I wanted? It must be me; there must be something else.

I I I

I spent almost two years feeling frustrated and angry and hurt after my divorce. I always attempted to take the higher consciousness road (and failed most of the time), but I often focused on seeing my own failures in why my ex-husband and I could not get along, why our divorce was so ghastly, and why we fought so brutally. I blamed myself over and over again, as if I was somehow responsible for the way he was behaving and I could somehow change it. As if I could somehow change him. He wasn't being what I wanted him to be—why couldn't I control him?

When we grab hold of the notion that we create our reality, we begin to see ourselves as the masters of the universe, the ultimate puppeteers, and to some degree we are, but it's important to know whose strings we actually strum. One morning not too long ago, after living in my own hole of blame and disappointment at my failure to manipulate my puppets, I woke up and it hit me. I could manipulate him, but not by assuming I had created him and therefore held the strings. He was his own creation and I was mine. I began to focus on my own movements, my own steps, and let him do his own dance. It was a dance that hadn't changed, at least not that I could tell, but my perception of it had and therefore so had my reality around it. I changed my language from asshole to human, flawed human, like me. I found compassion instead of anger. I stopped making it about me and realized he had his own set of rules he was living by.

It's more than just rearranging the furniture. It's an actual paradigm shift, so to speak. There is no magical poof where the walls disappear and the car in the driveway morphs into a Porsche. It's a perceptual shift with same walls and same car, but a different perspective. Not reality bending—perception bending.

I had been seeing my ex-husband as an asshole, so that's what he was being. Once I stopped seeing him that way, he stopped too. Because we have kids, he will be in my life for a long time. I can either spend the next twenty years dealing with an asshole while he deals with a person he perceives to be a controlling bitch, or I can get practical. Whenever I have to deal with something relating to our life, I get very clear on the outcome I desire, why I desire it, and from what perspective I am having that desire, and I decide if it is really necessary. When I do that, and do it for real and not half-assed, everything seems to work out exactly as I intended. No fights, no drama, no ass-hole or bitch. Just the facts, ma'am.

So there you go—I do create my reality. I just wish I could figure out how to find Ryan Gosling.

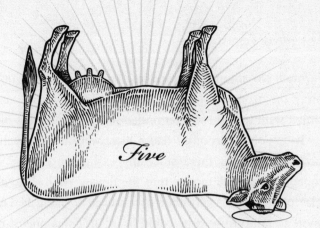

To Attach or Not to Attach—
That Is the Question

Moving is often listed as one of the top five most stressful things people experience in their lives, along with dealing with death, planning weddings, work, and marriage/relationship issues. I've done all of those things too many times to count. You'd think by now I'd be an expert at managing the stress.

Just this year, I moved from the house I shared with my ex-husband and kids to a new house. It was time to get a new place, with new energy, new walls to hang new pictures on, and a new bed that didn't hold the vibrations of a marriage in turmoil. No amount of smudging or energy work would clear away the aroma of failure from my old bedroom, and every time I went to bed I was reminded that I had failed at marriage.

In my old bedroom, I had a huge wall-hanging behind my bed. It had been there since my ex-husband and I hung it together when we moved into the house. We had giggled and playfully tickled each other as we tried to hang it. I was too short to hold it up so he could hook it. It was one of the final fun moments of intimacy we had together. It wasn't long after that the stress of kids, finances, and life covered over our love for each other until we couldn't see it anymore.

As I began the process of organizing and packing my old house to get ready for the move, I realized that it was probably time to let go of a lot of things I carried around, both inner and outer, material and emotional often neatly tied together with a bow. A knickknack, a picture, a platter, or some candlesticks—all the things we collect to remind us of the feeling we had when we picked up that snazzy set of ceramic pumpkin salt shakers.

For weeks before I moved, I went from room to room, closet to closet, slowly and methodically touching, smelling, gazing at each item, reliving the moment that thing was acquired. The little mosaic glass owl lamp I found while driving from California to Louisiana with my dog and a boyfriend (we had stopped at all the random antique stores along the way, and even though I didn't have much money on that trip, I bought that little owl lamp, so god-awful it was awesome). The reading monkey bookends my dad gave me, again classically ugly—Kitschy with a capital K. A gazillion little candle holders in every shape and size, all mixed together with every ceramic kitty my kids ever painted, every plaster of paris hand mold. Talk about sacred cows.

In one way or another, everything in my house had a story to go along with it, and for a long time I felt letting go of the thing would cause me to forget the memories, the feeling I had experienced. I had boxes and boxes of pictures from my wedding and wedding gifts handmade by old friends. Instead of traditional wedding gifts, we had asked for people to make us something shaped like a heart, which meant that I ended up with a box in my basement containing almost twenty little hearts in various sizes and materials. I wondered what I should do with this stuff.

My mother was moving into the new house with me, and I watched as she shed the last of the antique furniture my father had given her. She sold her car, which, even though she didn't drive it much anymore, meant independence and freedom to her. I wondered if one day I would experience that as an old lady, giving away the final bits and pieces of my material life, my independence. None of the stuff we acquire throughout our lives should matter, but it does. I'd be lying if I said it didn't.

Finally packed and ready for moving day, I was confronted by movers who eyed me, stunned, and told me they weren't sure if it was all going to fit into the truck—and this was no small truck, mind you. And here I thought I'd done a good job of letting go. The movers, who obviously knew more about the art of nonattachment than I did, clearly saw me as attached to my things. I felt judged.*

As the movers filled the truck with all the things I had deemed in my purging to still be of value, the things I was attached to,

I started to explore my understanding of the concepts of nonattachment and attachment. I didn't like feeling judged, and I didn't like feeling bad about loving things. What I found tipped the crap right out of those particular cows. Whammo! Now I have some pretty strong thoughts on the whole thing. Shocking, I know.

Once again I was faced with the contradiction of a concept and its practical application in my life. The struggle of trying to live a certain way, which was supposed to bring me more happiness, often made happiness feel farther away.

After ensconcing myself in the New Age world, this idea that we mustn't be attached really stung me. As I have said about a million times already in this book, I like shoes, I like things. Moving for me was never an easy undertaking. Most twenty- or thirtysomethings can manage with a nice little truck and a couple of friends—not me. I was in there with the forty-footer and the moving crew, so when I first encountered this whole nonattachment concept, I judged myself harshly on my failure to master the art of nonattachment. And when the movers stated that I had too much stuff, well, that was the straw that tipped the last cow for me, because who is anyone to decide how much stuff you can have? It isn't the stuff; it's how you deal with the stuff. It's how the stuff exists in your life that matters.

This is what Wikipedia says about detachment: "Detachment, also expressed as nonattachment, is a state in which a person overcomes his or her attachment to desire for things, people or concepts of the world and thus attains a heightened perspective."†

And I thought my three-inch heels were giving me a higher perspective (bad pun score). Well, I guess I was wrong.

Again this is an Eastern concept, mainly from Buddhism. For the record, I don't mean to pick on Buddhism, but you have to admit that most of our spiritual practices were brought over from there along with those nifty red lacquered armoires. It's not Buddhism's fault we Westerners take things way too seriously or literally. We're too busy to read the fine print. In my opinion, most of us need quick-fix answers to everything and often don't take time to really understand the history and nuances of a concept (maybe I'm just talking to myself—but probably not). But, as happens with many New Age tenets, being attached was somehow made bad. Ironic how a whole philosophy based on nonjudgment judged a lot of things as bad or good and filled me with a lot of rules about how I should be living in order to be happy. Boy, this happiness thing is a lot of work.

For many of us, nonattachment has become code for ignore it (insert here whatever it is you desire, but don't want to admit to desiring because you might seem attached to it and therefore less spiritual) and pretend it doesn't matter, even though it probably does, because otherwise you wouldn't want it.

In Buddhism and many other spiritual ideologies, attachment equals suffering, so nonattachment equals happy life. Um, so if I just walk around not caring about anything, loudly saying that I'm not attached so others will look at me in awe at my very spiritual way of living, letting it all blow in the wind, and just accepting everything as it appears in the moment, I'll be happy? If I detach myself from my Manolos, all I'm going to be is three inches shorter, and we all know I have body issues!

If I hear one more person tell me how they are not attached to the outcome, I'm going to throw my copy of *Zen and the Art of Motorcycle Maintenance* at them. Because really, you're attached.

I seriously read somewhere that when you're nonattached, all you can be is love. How is that possible? If you're not attached to anything, how can you love it? Isn't loving it being attached to it? Oh yeah, I suppose they're talking about that eternal all-being love. I'm not even sure that's possible, let alone something I want to be. Don't get me wrong, all loving is a great concept, but to me it reeks of manure, cow manure in fact. It reeks of should-do and should-be and pressure to achieve, and I've done enough of the overachieving thing. The idea of being nonattached is a cow I've been really attached to tipping over.

When I tried to live nonattachment, I felt deprived, victimized, and eventually bitter about what it was I wasn't allowing myself to have or desire. People can be downright judgmental, and I have always been concerned about what other people think, especially my peers. I'm being silly here, but I realized that while writing about being attached to my shoes was mostly just a joke, in fact I was attached because I cared about how I looked. I cared about it because I hated the way I looked, and my shoes helped me feel better about myself. So it wasn't really the shoes, it was the feeling my shoes gave me.

I challenge anyone reading this right now to not be attached to, say, your cell phone in a blizzard. Okay, maybe some people wouldn't be, but honestly ask yourself: what are you so attached to that you can't possibly live without it? Can you love without being attached? Really, think about it. I'll wait.

Come on, it's not hard. Mostly.

Maybe we should start with what attachment is and what the concept of nonattachment really means.

Is attachment greed? Is it need? Is it being in love with someone, or is it craving something so much that you actually feel you can't live without it? Don't be shy—no one is listening.

Hey, I know: let's play I'm Attached! Now it's time to list all the things you're really attached to. I'll go first:

Hi, my name is Betsy, and I'm attached to those chocolate chip cookie volcano cakes you get at the store, but not for long because they're impermanent and will soon only be a figment, a memory. Therefore I will suffer because of the loss of the taste of the chocolate and the addition of inches to my hips. Double suffering to go along with my double scoop. Yum!

I am attached to my shoes (already admitted that, and yes, I have a couple pairs that I would truly suffer over).

I'm attached to cigarettes and coffee in the same fanatical way first-graders are attached to their BFFs. I'm attached to that morning cup and puff, and even at midnight, when caffeine is probably going to keep me awake, I'm attached to it. Let's face it—if you're up at midnight drinking coffee and smoking, you're not going to sleep anyway, so you might as well enjoy being awake. And since no one else is up, you might as well hang out with your BFFs. They don't talk back, and they always agree with you, and I'm attached to being agreed with too, so it's an awesome double (or is that triple?) shot of attachment.

I am attached to my friends (my real live ones, the ones who talk back), some of whom are far away from me. Sometimes I miss them so much I feel like I could die (okay, maybe that's a bit dramatic, but I suffer for sure).

I am attached to my family. They may be dysfunctional and crazy, but gosh I really love those nut jobs and would suffer if they were gone.

I am attached to my owl lamp and my monkey bookends.

I am attached to fulfilling my dreams (ooh, that's a biggie).

So attachment is anything you want so badly that you'd be sad if it was gone. You'd suffer, and no one really likes to suffer. Our desire to avoid suffering is probably why somewhere along the path to enlightenment someone said attachment is bad because suffering is bad. But isn't suffering on some level necessary? Can't suffering be a good thing?

By this point, you're probably used to me being a bit absurd in my analogies. The goal here is to have fun, maybe even laugh a little, even when we're talking about suffering. One of my biggest cows I've tipped over was the idea that I had to be a certain way about everything, because if I wasn't, somehow I wasn't spiritual, in which case I'd never be happy, and if I wasn't happy, I was going to suffer.

Since when did suffering get such a bad rap? How about, suffering is a feeling, and feeling is living. When we can allow ourselves to feel the depths of each experience, the permission to feel the loss, to suffer, to grieve, we are living. That is an important piece of our happiness puzzle, because if you can't grieve, you can't move on, and if you can't move on, you won't be happy. The trick is not to get stuck grieving—that's attachment. Every step is part of the process, and if you skip a step, or get stuck on one, you're attached to that experience, even addicted to it, because it's obviously giving you something; otherwise you wouldn't be attached to it.

In Buddhism, the four noble truths say that life equals suffering because basically we forget that everything is transient. We forget that nothing is permanent, even suffering. Joy is fleeting like the emotional experience of the bliss of your first kiss. Once we have that experience, we spend the rest of our lives chasing it. We love things like that red race car and how cool we feel while we're driving it, so when it's repossessed, we're definitely going to suffer. We're attached to that feeling we get when that guy calls because it tells us we're loved, and we can't get that feeling unless he calls. We are even attached to our "self." I mean, if there weren't a "you," how could you be attached to that shiny red car? We forget the "self" is a delusion, because basically there is no self. There is just your perception of you, an imagined entity that is forever wandering on the wheel of becoming . . . okay, what?!

A moment ago I listed a whole bunch of things I'm attached to, but the truth is I'm really not attached to those things; I just think I am because I believe I am. Really, it all boils down to what you believe. It's super easy to create a belief that the things we think we're attached to are important because we are attached to the feelings these outside things give us, mostly because we believe those feelings aren't within us. You see these things as separate from you, as objects that bring you joy, when in fact, anything can bring you joy if you let it. It's not the owl lamp that is making me happy, it's that every time I turn that baby on and its little beady eyes light, it reminds me of that feeling of pure joy I had. It also reminds me that even though that feeling is from my past, I can experience it again and again and again, even if I'm suffering over something else.

Okay, that's easy. We can all understand that things are just things, and we can let go of our attachment to them pretty easily. Even though I swear to God there are some shoes that I am convinced were brought here by angels to remind us that we are loved. Anyway, I digress. I will work on letting go of my attachment to certain things.

But what about our dreams and things that are seemingly intangible? Attachments have two components: emotional need and soul's desire. Emotional needs should be dealt with. You should really dig down to the bottom of why you have that emotional need, because usually that's where the suffering will really wreak havoc. An emotional need left hanging about will never be fulfilled, and then you're stuck in attachment. But if you clean up the emotional need that's mucking up the window, you will be able to clearly see the path to your soul's desire. Your soul's desire is also insatiable but, at least to me, having something to be attached to is what drives you. You'll be able to find joy in exploring ways to reach it, and there will be no "suffering," although there might be some cold dark nights when you're curled up alone with your teddy bear.

I have a dream. I have a desire to create something, and I'm attached to seeing it through. I dreamed of writing this book. I wanted a book deal badly. Why? Because it validated that I had something to say and that someone agreed with me; it meant that I was worthy (emotional need). But also because I felt so strongly that what I had to say would mean something to someone and to me. I felt that writing this book would help me find a piece of me I knew was there but couldn't see, and I hoped that it would be of service to someone else going through the same things I had. My soul's desire is to help people see their own way to being happy and fulfilled.

Take a moment to think about what your true dream is. You will probably find that some of it is attached to emotional needs based on old beliefs, but underneath all the stinky tennis shoes and broken stilettos, your soul's desire is there.

When I examined myself, I saw a lot of emotional need for validation, but underneath that need was a true desire to figure out how to live in this world, and once I did, to share that information. Writing books and making movies about what I've learned brings me the greatest joy, so that's my soul desire.

Does that mean I am going to suffer if it doesn't happen? Probably. But there is a nuance here that I often think is missed.

There is SUFFERING, as in feeling sadness or pain because of an experience that you truly lived and allowed yourself to feel, as in when you suffer the loss of a loved one, or like in my case, a divorce. I suffered for a while, I grieved, and it sucked, but then I allowed myself to move on. Your soul's desire has a way of always rising to the top, so when my soul's desire called to me in the midst of my suffering, I listened and followed.

And then there is suffering, as in everything in my life sucks because that guy didn't call and I'm ugly and no one will ever love me and my beautiful car just got repossessed and I stepped in dog poop. These are the kinds of suffering we get caught up in that really aren't worth our time. They may feel insurmountable at the time, but being attached to them only causes suffering and keeps you from reaching your soul's desire.

I think sometimes we confuse nonattachment with complacency, with this need to feel blissful all the time and to just be okay with everything. But that's not what nonattachment actually means. Because one cannot just be okay with everything, and if you say you are, well, you're lying to yourself. You're hiding behind the words *I'm not attached.*

For me, allowing myself to feel was like releasing myself from handcuffs worn all my life. I was so afraid to let anyone see me cry. I am strong and tough and very spiritual, God dammit, and I know that feelings and emotions tied to things in my life are just more of the illusion. It's all a lie, and I can simply laugh it off and move on to the next thing. Nothing penetrates me. (Bullshit.)

A few months after my divorce, I sent my kids off for a weekend with their dad. For some reason, that weekend proved tough for me. The weight of the situation, the realization that I would be doing this for the next fifteen years, hit me hard, and as they drove away, I crumbled to the ground right there in the middle of the sidewalk, sobbing for everyone to see. My neighbor came running over (for the record, he is super hot, and I am an ugly crier). He asked me what had happened, and in between the sobs and pointing in the direction my children had been driven off in, I did my best impersonation of a three-year-old who's just lost her favorite stuffy. I tried to explain the hole in my heart. After about five minutes of sobbing in the arms of almost a complete stranger, I composed myself and felt better. I felt the pain, sat with it (in the arms of a hot guy, which I think helped a lot), and released it. Finally, I went back into my house and had a really awesome weekend. I was actually able to enjoy that for forty-eight hours, I could do what I wanted, sleep in, eat when I wanted, and generally have some peace and quiet.

▌ ▐ ▌

Finding the balance between need and the soul's desire is key to nonattachment. I had an emotional need to know my kids loved me, but my soul's desire was for them to be happy, which meant spending time with their dad. When you have a passion, go for it, but remember that the external things that go along with that passion are not what fulfills you—they are not what brings you joy. It's the act of doing and being in the moment with it that brings those feelings, so enjoy them! And know that nothing is forever. Even you, even your passion, will change and grow and possibly expand—grow with it.

Starting with your "self," are you the same person you were five years ago? Really? In truth, you may have a lot of the same qualities and habits, and you have probably carried around a lot of the same beliefs for a long time, but with each moment, you're changing, so in reality you're not the same. Hell, even your cells are not the same ones you had seven years ago, so in truth you are not permanent, and nothing is.

Five years ago I was married, living in a different state, and had a whole set of plans and dreams equal to that life. Now we all know what happened to those plans, and for a while I believed all was lost. No house in the country, no perfect husband and family. How could I possibly live the life I thought I wanted? But after a lot of internal exploration into my attachments to that life, I realized that I could still have my soul's desire; I just needed to change some of the furniture (tip some cows and deal with my emotional needs). So out went a bunch of things that were attached to that emotional need. Bye-bye big wall-hanging behind my bed, bye-bye big man speakers, hello flowering, billowing duvet and curtains. And even those new things are just things, helping me paint my picture as I make my way to living my soul's desire, which never changed. They are just decorations I use to remind me of moments when I felt a certain way, to help me build my dream, but I am still the dreamer, monkey bookends or not.

Nonattachment does not equal nonfeeling, nonliving, non-experiencing. When you have a strong feeling of attachment to something, it's probably because in your own mind, you don't feel connected with it, or rather, the emotion it brings. You haven't done the emotional work needed to understand why you have that need. Maybe it's tied to your soul's desire, in which case, good. Clean it up and keep it. But if not, then it's emotional drama, and you should just get rid of it. I couldn't let go of that wall-hanging until I worked through the pain of my divorce, which, to be honest, I'm still working on, but I've done enough to finally let that thing go. And I did it my way, without anger—I didn't rip it into a million pieces with a butcher knife, frothing at the mouth and filled with rage and hurt. I simply took it down and gave it away, with a smile and a twinkle in my eye and a thanks for the memories in my heart. That is the art of living nonattachment: being attached, but not attached. It's in the understanding that you can find the love of it, the joy of it in the moment, but that you also accept that it does not make you and it does not bring you the happiness you seek. When you can say good-bye to that person, place, thing, time, or event with the gratitude for what it gave you in the moment—that's nonattachment.

I think you can agree with me that most things in life aren't forever. It took me a long time to get to that understanding. I can remember the days when I thought the pain would never go away or when I wanted that night to last forever, but they eventually both ended. It took a long time to find my own way to accept that, to find joy in riding the wave of life, to watch it come in and go out and to see what things it carried with it, and to let them in and let them go.

If you can live your life with the wisdom that nothing is forever, you can enjoy it while it lasts and say good-bye when it's time and look forward to the next thing.

That's a lot easier said than done, especially when it comes to people. For me it's my kids. We become very attached to the outcome of that story.

I can remember being pregnant and dreaming of my celestial child, my beautifully spiritual being born out of my body who would arrive speaking in Deepak Chopra quotes filled with the sagacity of her old-soul years. For three and a half years I played classical music (I even did this while she was in the womb). I filled her life with the divine, magical, mythical elements of water, fire, earth (and a couple of unicorns to boot). I bathed her little cherubic body in earthly organic substances. I grew her food and pureed it myself. I clothed her heavenly bum in the finest of biodegradable diapers. I let Mother Nature be her guide. Then, after a long day of merry play together with her blocks made from sustainable wood and painted with nontoxic paint, we were about to head upstairs for a cup of hand-churned frozen yogurt and I began to sing our song, "Clean up, clean up, everybody do their share," to which my little goddess of light turned to me and said promptly, "I wish I was older, and I could pay someone to do this." Suddenly, I had to let go of every dream I had about my light goddess daughter. I had to let go of the attachment to my story about who she was and realize that she was her own self, and that I could hold on to my attachment of what I wanted her to be and suffer, or I could love her for who she was and live in bliss watching her become her.

Just like that red race car, people often fulfill an emotional need within us, even as we love them with every ounce of our being. They change or we change, and suddenly they no longer fit into our lives.

Getting divorced and falling out of love is a surefire way to realize that nothing is forever. Remember when you thought it would be forever? You lay in his arms imagining yourself as an old couple, holding hands and walking through the park in Paris. Then one day that image blew up like a firecracker on the Fourth of July. You did a quick check to make sure all your fingers were still there, and sure enough, it felt like one was missing. The breakdown of love is probably the hardest thing we deal with. For a while, I spent a lot of time being mad at myself for falling in love with him. But thankfully, each morning, as I woke with eyes swollen from crying myself to sleep, I looked into the eyes of my son who climbed into bed with me every night. His eyes are just like my ex-husband's—surrounded by long gorgeous lashes, they're big and hazel brown and filled with love. I couldn't stay mad at my ex-husband or myself for falling in love, because for a while we were, and it was great, and I am so glad I had the opportunity to experience that. And look what came from it: two amazing kids who I cherish.

It was in my son's eyes that I learned nothing is forever, nothing is permanent, but this doesn't have to be a doomsday prophecy. Enjoy the moments you have with loved ones. Learn about yourself from them, laugh with them, and cry with them. Live with them and let them go when it's time and in gratitude. Because they, it, the people, places, and times in your life, they aren't really separate from you anyway. They are forever ingrained in your being; they are a part of you, so there's no need to yearn for them.

I promise, owl lamp or not, you're going to be okay.

So, to answer the question, to attach or not to attach—attach with a quick-release button.

Note

* George Carlin did an awesome bit about stuff and how we deal with it. It's worth checking out and gives a perspective on stuff, which I seem to have a lot of and have a hard time detaching from. http://www.youtube.com/watch?v=MvgN5gCuLac.

† Okay, okay. I know what you're thinking: "Wikipedia? Seriously, Betsy!" I do check around at other definitions and sources, and Wikipedia got it right this time. So, don't judge me!

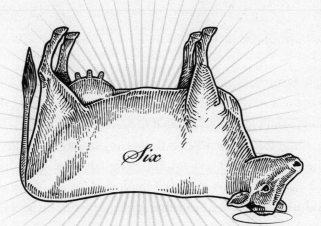

Who Is the Universe and Why Does It Have All My Stuff?

I share a lot about my kids. I am bracing myself for my daughter's teenage years when she reads this book and decides to use only her father's name as a way to separate herself from me and my stories about her youth. Hopefully when she's older she'll appreciate the gratitude I feel toward her and her brother for the wisdom they have brought me. For me, raising children has been one of the greatest opportunities to observe the human condition in action as it sets in, takes hold, and forever separates us from our true selves. Until, that is, we figure out that we probably knew more at five than we do now. One of the traits that never ceases to amaze me about my children is their innate ability to manifest what they want effortlessly.

Or at least it seems effortless. They simply wish upon a star and somehow that new toy, that play date, that candy bar from the check stand just appears. I think my kids are masters at this, and it's not because I'm some pushover who just gives in. I'm tough. I am a mom of steel as we stand at the checkout, and they beg and use every power they can wield against my steely "No." But I'll tell you right now, when I am looking for a parking space in a crowded parking lot, I tell them to put out their parking mojo, and sure enough, within seconds a parking spot opens.

Speaking of steel, my son fell in love with Superman and told me, all matter of fact, that the Easter Bunny was going to bring him a Superman doll. As a result, I searched high and low for a Superman doll, but with no luck. I mean, just about every other superhero you could imagine was available, but for some reason Superman hadn't had his turn in the mega blockbuster summer movie. (This was before the new Superman movie—now the dolls are a dime a dozen, and my son could care less. He is always ahead of his time.)

Anyway, one evening we went for a night out at a local shopping mall. It was an outdoor spectacle complete with its own free trolley ride that the kids could ride as much as they wanted. This mall had an old-style toy store, one that still stocked some of the oldies like Slinkys and retro Pez dispensers. I thought for sure they'd have an old Superman doll, but shockingly they didn't. They had every other oldie but goodie superhero, but no

Superman. I began crafting an easy letdown for my son, telling him the Easter Bunny might not be able to find a Superman doll and maybe he should think about something else. He looked at me like I was nuts and said in his little man voice, "Mom, seriously, the Easter Bunny is gonna come through."

So off we went to ride the trolley. As we rounded the bend toward the end of the ride, the conductor announced that the Easter Bunny had set up shop in the center of the mall and was taking visitors. My kids' eyes lit up, and they squealed with delight. Ugh, I thought. There goes forty bucks on a picture with a bunny in a bad suit, but I couldn't say no to those little faces, so we dismounted our trolley chariot, and they went running straight for the little house all Eastered out with spring colors and eggs and whatever else the Easter Bunny has at his cottage. Although not out of sight, they were all the way across the court when I heard my son shout, "MOM, MOM, OH MY GOD!" I wasn't sure if it was a fearful shout—like the Easter Bunny's head had fallen off and my little Max would be forever scarred, wondering if all mystical beings had human heads underneath their own—or if something cool had happened.

I ran to him, and as I approached, I was stunned. My mouth dropped open, and I stopped dead in my tracks as he stood there in front of the Easter Bunny's door holding a Superman doll. He was dancing a jig and screaming, "I told you, Mom! I told you the Easter Bunny would bring me a doll." I just stood there and said, "Yes, Max, yes, you did. Now, can you ask the Easter Bunny for like a million dollars, a BMW, and a really hot, emotionally available, independently wealthy man while you're at it?"

Okay, so here's how it happened. Outside the Easter Bunny cottage was one of those little carts you see at malls these days, like little mini-stores usually selling sea salt from the Dead Sea or phone covers, only this one had toys. It wasn't actually part of the Easter Bunny display, but it was just close enough to look like it to a five-year-old, and who am I to argue? As the kids went in to see the Bunny, I asked the cart keeper how much. He said, "You know, I don't know. I only have one of those things— it's the only one I got, and I just got it today." And that, my friends, is how it is supposed to work, or so I'm told. As I stood there watching my son snuggle his Superman doll and hug the Easter Bunny, I felt pure love and gratitude. I wondered how come I couldn't do that.

I have spent many a night sitting on my porch swing, looking up into the vast universe, asking, begging, desiring, and wanting stuff. Just for clarity, when I say stuff, I don't just mean those Jimmy Choos. I also mean the transcendental stuff like peace and wisdom and happiness and love and all the other "stuff" we want. It's all stuff, and we all want it, and for some reason we can't seem to get it without help from the cosmos. When we do get it, we spiritual folks say, "The universe provided."

Which brings up the question, Who or what is the universe, and why does it have all my stuff? Okay, seriously, who the fuck is the universe, and how the hell did it just drop a Superman doll into my son's hand? And why do I expect it to answer all of my requests and prayers as if it's some sort of divine vending machine?

Here's what Wikipedia says about the universe: "The Universe is commonly defined as the totality of existence including planets, stars, galaxies, the contents of intergalactic space, and all matter and energy. Definitions and usage vary and similar terms include the cosmos, the world, and nature."

Okay, so that's big. Totality of existence pretty much means everything. In the YouTube video "The Most Astounding Fact," Neil deGrasse Tyson, in voiceover, reminds us that we have something in common with the universe. We're made up of the same specs of energy, of matter. Which means (if you didn't get it with the totality-of-existence definition) we are essentially a part of the universe.[*1]

Anyway, if I'm a part of the universe, am I asking myself for all this stuff? And if I am asking myself, then why am I torturing myself? Give it up, woman! Apparently my kids already get this, which is why a Superman doll can appear out of thin air from the Easter Bunny. Maybe the Easter Bunny is the universe. Maybe whoever told me the Bunny wasn't real was wrong.

Once, before I was I and you were you, we were. Yep, we were. The story goes that we were the totality of existence. We played in the sea of potentials just being love and light, but apparently that got boring and someone, something, some prism of light in our little bubble of joy and love, got the bright idea that maybe we should give suffering and separateness a try—so BOOM went a big bang. Through years and years and millennia after millennia, our divineness grew into the beings of misery and suffering that we are today. Or aliens made us— it depends on who you ask. Either way, we're an unhappy bunch for the most part.

Why are we so unhappy? Well, let me ask you: if you were wrapped in a warm blanket of love pretty much 24/7 and then all of a sudden you weren't, wouldn't you be unhappy? But here's the catch. When we exploded into a bazillion little specs of light, we forgot something really important. We forgot that we still are a part of that totality of existence. We are a part of that love being that wanted to experience something other than joy all the time, so we popped the big cherry and here we are. This reality is our canvas. We are the creators of our lives, the painters of this masterpiece, and we get to paint it however we want.

In the beginning of one of my favorite movies, *People v. The State of Illusion*, Austin Vickers describes our lives as a mosaic created by us. We are the artists, and the canvas, if you will, is the universe. "It's our Etch A Sketch," he says.[2] It's our playing field, and we have the power to put on it whatever we want. So why don't we? I mean, I don't know about you, but if I had a dollar for every time I've prostrated to that illusive universe, begging and pleading for something, I would probably have enough money to buy it.

But if the universe is an Etch A Sketch, an empty canvas, and I am the artist, then it is me I am groveling to, it is me I am begging to give me that which I seek. If I'm seeking it, I'm telling myself I don't have it. Well, of course I don't have it! Otherwise, why would I be asking for it? Let me try saying this straight: if I am part of the universe and I ask the universe for a new pair of shoes, I am essentially asking myself for a new pair of shoes. (To be fair to the universe, which is me, I often give myself those shoes. Shoes are easy. It's peace and happiness I seem to hold out on.)

The idea that I am the universe, or at least a piece of it, and that I am somehow, like Mary Poppins, carrying around a bag filled with answers to desires and wants, has always frustrated me. I mean, clearly, if I did have that bag, I would surely dig into it. It took a while, but I finally realized that I have been asking myself for all the wrong things. I cannot paint that which I don't truly desire, and while those Jimmy Choos are sexy and hot, I know deep inside they won't fulfill me. I've painted that picture many times in my life, and I know what it looks like.

Again, we've come back to what are we asking for and why. Will that person, place, thing, or event actually give us what we are truly looking for, and why do you think you don't already have it? I've touched a bit here and there on the idea of separation. In attachment, separation is what makes us feel the need to get something when really, if it's truly our soul's desire, then it is a part of us, and therefore we already have it. No need to ask, just look and it's there. If I don't seem to have what I'm looking for, then I can honestly say it's probably because either I don't really want it (it's not my soul's desire) or I'm asking for the wrong thing.

This is one of those nebulous "can't touch it, can't really see it" concepts—that is, until you finally do feel it for yourself. My son wanted that Superman doll, and he saw no reason he couldn't have it. He knew that doll with all his being. He described it to me; he told me it would be soft so he could sleep with it, but it would have a lifelike face so that when he played with it, it would look real. There wasn't a doubt in his mind about any of this. When I told him that the Easter Bunny might not bring it to him, he assured me that the Easter Bunny would. But he also said to me that if the Easter Bunny failed to come through, he would get it for his birthday. My son was patient, and he wasn't about to let his nonbelieving, bubble bursting mama rain on his parade. He knew he was connected to that Superman doll. It was his already, and how it landed in his arms didn't really matter.

This concept of connectedness eluded me for a long time because I never really felt connected to anything. I couldn't grasp that intangible idea. I kept looking for connection and couldn't find it. What I finally realized was that I couldn't feel connected to a life that wasn't my soul's desire. I couldn't feel connected to things that truly wouldn't serve my true self. I needed to clean my pasture and begin to ask for my piece of the universe from that cleaned self, not from the self that was bogged down in old beliefs about what I thought I was supposed to be asking.

Austin Vickers, besides being an awesome filmmaker, is an amazing yoga instructor. He told me about a yoga term *leela*, which means divine play. It can refer to children at play or to a divine story that is unfolding with me as its director. It's like the blank canvas, and I am its painter. But how can I find the true colors that speak to me, the me who resides underneath all the beliefs, all the ideas about what is right?

So much of what I have written about in this book is about finding the core of your being, that place where everything outside you doesn't matter because you already have everything you need inside. That is probably one of the hardest things I have come to accept, that there is nothing out there, no shoes (can you imagine!), no man, nothing that will actually give me happiness and peace. When I can let go of the needs I've been programmed to think I need based on beliefs that aren't true or don't really fit, when I can forgive myself for the past where I failed and fumbled because I didn't know who I was, when I can see that the car I have gets me where I want to go (oh, and by the way, thank God I don't have the shiny BMW because have you ever been in the backseat of a car that generally transports kids? That is not a pretty sight!), that's it. That is peace, that is happiness, that is my universe giving me what I truly desire. See, I (the true self, the capital I) know that right now that shiny BMW isn't what I really want, it's what I think I need in order to fulfill my need to feel good about myself. But I am good without it, because if I had that car, I'd be stressing about the string cheese and cheddar bunnies. The real *I* has already given me the peace I have been begging the universe (me, in case you forgot) for because the real *I* knows that no matter what snack foods end up in the backseat of the car I already have, it's going to be fine.

My son loves his stuffed buddies. They're his comfort, and he has a vast menagerie of friends he cuddles with at night. It's his way of finding peace now that he sleeps in his big boy bed, even though he still usually finds his way into mine along with every one of his sleeping buddies, including Superman (I have often rolled over and found Superman between my boobs).

My ex-husband has a Superman shirt, and we bought one for Max, and they used to wear their shirts at the same time. Max was so proud to wear that shirt, and when it finally didn't fit anymore, there were tears all around. I kept it in his keepsake box. The quest for the Superman doll began shortly after my ex-husband and I separated and he moved out of the house our family shared. For months my son worried that we might not be safe enough without a superhero (or his dad) to save us from some sort of impending doom. In other words, it wasn't really a toy he was after; he wanted to be able to sleep with his dad every night. It was his soul's desire, and if he couldn't have the real thing, then a Superman doll would do and nothing was going to stop him from getting one, not even the Easter Bunny.

I was amazed to watch how my son created an attachment to an outside "thing," a doll, to fulfill his need for safety and comfort. He was five, and grasping the bigger concept that he had that safety without the doll was a bit much for him. His soul's desire was to feel safe and comforted in a tough time, and he manifested what he truly needed to get that feeling, and yes, it was a thing. As I realized this, I began to tell him as often as I could how loved he was, how his dad was never truly away from him, and that he could simply think of him and feel him there, even if his Superman doll wasn't with him. Since that time, Superman has found his way to the drawer with all of Max's other buddies. They're not completely out of reach, but Max also knows that the love and comfort he needs are within him and around him.

Note

* On a side note: Neil is so going to be pissed that I mentioned his name in this book. He's a hard-core atheist and reductionist (a reductionist is someone who believes that the universe and everything in it can be figured out and defined using Newtonian physics, sort of like "There's an app for that," only they say "There's an equation for that," and believes that the love, the dreams, the weird déjà vu you experienced last week were all just whoopsies in the brain). So let's just say that we have opposing views, and our groups don't always get along. But this "The Most Astonishing Fact" YouTube thing rocks no matter which way you swing on the spiritual-atheist metronome.

"Feel," Another Four-Letter Word

Sometimes you just want to throttle someone, and clearly we can't do that. Or can we? I ask coyly and rhetorically. Maybe if not literally, then at least in our heads for just a minute. Please? How often have we said no, we must rise above, be greater, more spiritual, and shove that baby deep down like a hot dog in a hot dog eating contest? I caught myself the other day, judging and reacting in horror as my sweet, loving eight-year-old explained how she really was mad at someone and wished they were never born. Of course this went against every image I had of my sweet, aware, conscious little wonder and I went into a long lecture about how she needed to be understanding, how wishing that upon someone would only bring her unhappiness, the whole trip, when really all she wanted was to be mad and hurt and feel it, express it, and get it out. And there I was telling her to shove it way down.

There goes another hot dog, piling up with all the rest until the inevitable upchuck involving barely chewed meat, bun, and condiments, landing all over us and anyone standing nearby. Spewing, I believe it is called, which is appropriately a word that can metaphorically also stretch from hot-dog–eating contests to how we vent something like anger.

I have come to a place where I am over this notion that spiritual means we mustn't feel "bad" feelings, we mustn't attach, we mustn't react. Which you know is not a good way to go, because the word *mustn't* is involved. I'm also not keen on this whole idea that we should love everybody, even if they are assholes. Maybe it's true that their asshole-ish tendencies and the shit that arises from those tendencies are all our fault because we created the situation so we could teach ourselves some lesson about our big, bad ego. And maybe we should just kill off our egos so we can live like eunuchs in caves, eventually floating so high that our astral bodies soar into the sky, bursting open like amethyst-colored firecrackers, sprinkling our love and light back onto the people (including the assholes) who haven't figured it all out and therefore deserve to suffer. But, seriously, if I hear one more of my compadres in the spiritual know-it-all circle say, "I wish they'd all wake up," I'm going to rip off their sleep masks and blind them with the light within me. Because we all could use a refresher course in emotional intelligence, and even the most bright-eyed and bushy-tailed beings among us are still asleep most of the time. Bad feelings and attachment and reactions are not automatically bad things.

The reality is, we're here in this reality, and we can either pretend it doesn't exist or master it. I'm going for mastery, but not in the way modern-day spirituality has offered up. It's time for a revolution in terms of what it means to live a spiritual life. I've said this before, but it bears repeating—life is spiritual and everything you do is spiritual. Period. The question isn't what is spiritual, or how do I live a spiritual life. You're living it. The question is, are you living the life you want, and if you're not, then what are you going to do to achieve it?

One the biggest fallacies in terms of what it means to be spiritual is this notion that emotions are bad, emotions are what bring you down, emotions cause suffering. *Feel* is a four-letter word, and when you utter the words "*I feel*" you get the all-knowing, slow nod from the spiritual high achievers. And ah-ha! You're feeling again! Most of us have been taught from an early age to hide how we feel so as not to offend anyone else's emotions. We live in a world where we spend a lot of time not saying what we want to say and hiding how we feel because it's not politically correct. On the flip side, we spend a lot of time being offended by what other people do or say to us. Well, here's a little unconditional love for you: it's time to get over it.

You're probably asking, Okay, then what exactly do you suggest I do to get over it? First, gain an understanding of how your emotions work or how you choose your emotional responses. You now know how your brain works in terms of attaching meanings to your experiences and that your brain generates a chemical with each of those experiences, which triggers an emotional response. So, we consider that we are basically big walking containers of chemicals and that, until you can get hold of managing how those chemicals are dispersed, you can mediate 'til the cows come home and it won't matter. Essentially we are drug addicts, and our drugs are our emotions.

Candace Pert wrote the quintessential book on this subject, and when I read it, it blew my mind.[1] *Molecules of Emotion* should be required reading for every teenager on the planet. In it, she describes how our emotions work. Basically, each emotion has a chemical related to it that is released in the brain—a peptide. These peptides, once released, cascade through our bodies like a shower of gold coins raining down from the heavens. It feels so good, our bodies just love it and can't get enough of it. After a lifetime of being fed a smorgasbord of candied juices, our bodies start to kind of like one flavor over the other, and like sneaking into that pile of Hershey bars you're hiding from your kids, we begin to seek out ways to feed our little addiction. Like anyone with an addiction, after a while we're not so shy about getting our fix and that fix requires more and more juice to be satiated.[2]

When I began to examine my past in terms of the concept of being addicted to my emotional response to life, it wasn't hard to find the pattern. I was addicted to praise and big shows of affection. I fell hard for any guy who told me I was pretty or sent me flowers. I was instantly in love, often without reading the fine print. Why? Because I always felt unworthy of love, not good enough, not smart enough, not tall enough (there's those body issues again), so being told I was those things fed me. Well, it fed my ego anyway.

As long as my ego got the drugs, my body learned to crave all that was good in the world. It didn't matter if it was true, or if the person feeding my ego's insatiable appetite was actually feeding his own emotional addictions. It was good enough to feed the need, and that's all that really mattered. But as you can with any muddy hole, you can dump as much water in it as you want, but it's going to evaporate and you're going to need more. Because in truth I didn't believe that anyone loved me, no matter how many visits I got from 1-800Flowers.com. I was still hungry because my stomach was vast, and mixed in with a hunger for love was a belief that ultimately the pretend love would disappear and betrayal and disappointment would step up to the table. I know it sounds convoluted, but we humans are complicated creatures. Our brains are a tangled web of elaborate connections, love wired with disappointment, success wired with fear of failure and survival, and on and on. Our job is to unwire all those zigzagging connections and create a more direct trip. Love equals love. Now wouldn't that make life a whole lot easier!

I spent an entire month writing down my emotional responses to my experiences from lots of different places in my life. There, in black and white, was my list. First, unsubstantiated love, followed by anger, frustration, and betrayal, all tied to the people, places, and things in my life I bought in order to feed my emotional addiction. Hell, I could feel betrayed at the grocery store when they were out of my favorite thumbprint cookies, as if somehow Trader Joe's was conspiring against me and my need for happiness, which could only be found after eating an entire box in one sitting. Damn them! Trying this type of list-making means you will be gifted with a pretty clear (and somewhat horrifying and daunting, because jeez, really? That many?) picture of your pattern of emotional addictions. If you compare it against your list of beliefs, you will see how you picked up those nasty little addictions.

And just like you would quit any habit, you work at it. You interrupt the pattern. Emotions are tied to your beliefs about yourself, the world, and chocolate (because, isn't everything?). Doing the work of uncovering your beliefs and the emotions attached to them will bring you awareness about who you are being.

There is a big word in the realm of spirituality: *consciousness*. Before worrying about the big idea of consciousness, let's just focus on your own for a moment. Most of the choices we make are pretty unconscious. They are learned responses repeated over time until we no longer even realize why we are making the choices we do.

I noticed I would often set myself up for disappointment by creating a need for someone to tell me how good I was, only to have them not fulfill that need (I'm still working on this, by the way). I figured this out by being conscious of my actions, by being present to my behavior and my body. I could actually feel the anticipation of getting a fix, like a heroin addict tying the knot. But every heroin addict knows deep down inside that the high is going to fade away, and deep down inside I knew that while the immediate feeling would feel good, there was a crash coming right behind it.

Dating after divorce is a surefire way for me to feed my emotional addiction and my belief that I am not worthy of love.
When my marriage failed, the belief that I was unworthy hit me
hard, so I started chasing men who would feed that feeling, that
addiction. I chose men who wouldn't actually love me, just so I
could feed my beast and be right about my belief. In choosing
my men, I overdosed on the drug of righteousness—I was right
after all these years: I am not lovable! See it's true, I've proven it.
Our egos love to be right, and our emotions give us the high we
so desperately crave, and sadly, we continue on with this until
we become aware of how we're torturing ourselves. After too
many nights of hailing a cab after walking out a strange door, or
doing the walk of shame to my car in a neighborhood I didn't
know, I realized that this addiction would never be satisfied
unless I quit cold turkey.

Becoming aware is a huge step toward working through the
addiction. I put myself on an emotional roller-coaster ride
because of the beliefs I created, and I allowed my ego to hide
my beliefs from me and be my wingman in the setup of my
eventual fall. Becoming aware is the way to get off the ride, so
now I am conscious of it. I am aware of it. I have woken up a bit
(but I'm still sleepy eyed). Still, every once in a while I catch
myself standing in that line, waiting for the needle and the
eventual highs and lows it brings.

As you become aware, give yourself a break; habits that have
taken forty-three years (in my case) to formulate will not go
away overnight. Withdrawals are tough, and while you may not
suffer the shakes, you're certainly going to fall off the wagon, a
lot. Each time you do, just be aware of it, be conscious of it, see

the cycle you created, the steps you took to get there. Make a note of it, observe it, if you will, and eventually it will become a less nagging need. You'll start catching yourself earlier in your process. Eventually, you'll be able to step out of line and let someone else go ahead of you, and hopefully, at some point, you won't need to get in line at all.

This is why I've started to play with the idea of allowing myself to feel. Okay, so maybe I don't let myself get so angry that I want to punch out my neighbors when they park their cars too close to my driveway. I have created a little practice that allows my emotions to process. The science on all of this reveals to us that an emotion, once triggered, takes about ninety seconds to complete its travels through your body. So give yourself ninety seconds—count, chant, breathe, punch a pillow—but give yourself the time. Then after the ninety seconds are up, it's up to you—do you want to keep feeling that way? You can use that time to bring your awareness out of hibernation. Through awareness of who you have been, you can make space for who you want to be. You can become conscious of other choices you might want to make and, as a master of your house of emotions, you can find your way to being who you want. I think, from a really common-sense take on it, it's about giving yourself time to choose your response from a more "conscious" perspective.

So remember, that wonderful chemical cascade of peptides lasts for about ninety seconds. After that rush, we can choose to continue feeling it, or we can choose to push that plate away and save room for dessert. The mistake we often make in caring for our emotional selves is that we don't allow ourselves to feel. Alternately, some of us feel too much. We feed on the smorgasbord of emotional drama like we're in Vegas at the five-dollar, all-you-can-eat buffet. Once you have mastered your emotions, you will find a whole new freedom in actually experiencing the beauty of your emotions, the gifts they give you, because instead of them running you, you will be the girl (or guy) in charge of them. Delight in the joy, revel in the sorrow, but do it consciously. It may be that you want to feel a particular way for more than ninety seconds. Okay, why is that? I have begun a whole new conversation with myself in these moments. For a lot of us, there is a cacophony of voices muttering in our heads, yammering on about our silly beliefs or telling us how to act and what to believe. Someone needs to corral that bunch, and that someone is you—your inner you, that voice of reason, the real reason, not the loud one who always talks over everyone else and pretends to have it all figured out. The voice that helps you remember why it is you're responding with a certain emotion, your conscious self who has a bird's-eye view of how you ended up connecting love with hurt and guides you back to connecting love with love.

During my divorce, I lived in a space where every time I walked out of the courtroom I was stunned, shocked, and really angry. I railed in my head against the injustice of it all. As I made my way to the car, I'd start in on myself, playing the game of pretending, putting on my mask of enlightened master and trying to tell myself that the universe had other plans, that there was a lesson in this moment for me and that I should find love and compassion. As I said these things, I would feel myself shoving my emotions deep down, professing to myself that they were just an illusion, and I could ignore them and they would go away, because I was "love," right?

I would sit in my car and look out the window. My divorce was no illusion, and even if it was, I was right in the middle of it. Sure, I could pretend, but where has that gotten me so far? Once, while sitting in my car, full-up with all of the emotion of the exquisite pain of the realness of what was happening to me, I began to sob and beat my steering wheel. I cried all the way home, and I cried for almost ten hours straight. At times, I played My Life Sucks and wore my victim mask with pride. I gave myself the room to be every emotion I wanted to be and in doing so, released them. I checked in every ninety seconds and said yes, keep going, you've held this in for a very long time, and it's going to take a while to purge it. I started my descent into darkness with the belief that all was lost, because in that moment it was.

After several hours, I fell to the floor in exhaustion. In my fall down the rabbit hole, I found beliefs tied up with my emotions. I saw the road map of hurt and disappointment that led me to become addicted to the emotions, convoluted as they were. There were contradictions at first, but eventually I saw it all come together, the puzzle that is me. I slept, and for the first time in a long time, I slept dreamlessly through the night. Everything I had was out and on the floor, and there was nothing left inside my head to pursue me into the land of my dreams or disturb my sleep. When I awoke, the feeling of failure was gone, the little pieces all connected, and I saw how I had come to be who I was. The fear had evaporated, the confusion was gone, and I began the business of picking up the pieces and finding something new to make of them.

In my humble opinion, besides *Molecules of Emotions*, the best work written on this subject comes from Dr. Joe Dispenza, who wrote the foreword for this book. His book *Breaking the Habit of Being Yourself* is another that should be required reading. If all of humanity simply understood this one concept, I imagine the world would probably be a very different place. You are addicted to your emotions because you've created a belief system around feeding them, and you can either keep doing the same thing, or you can become the master of them.

Dr. Joe describes a process that is very logical. We do it all the time when we want to quit smoking or drinking, or when we want to give up any other worldly addiction we have picked up. It's the same with our emotions. Our emotions aren't bad; they are a gift, a way to experience the reality, the illusion. They become bad because we judge them. Our society has decided being angry is bad. It has also decided that being sad requires more drugs, but in taking them, we never take the time to find the source of the emotions because we don't let them out long enough to see them through. In starving ourselves, in forbidding ourselves to feel, we have created a monster of addiction, an addiction that will be fed with us or without us. We become unaware of our own processes and stand around dumbfounded, wondering why our life is the way it is and why we don't have any control over it. Dr. Joe describes a process in which you first observe and understand. Once you've done that, you forgive and let go and then slowly and deliberately begin to interrupt your pattern. You don't interrupt the pattern by forcing it aside, but by exercising conscious observation and compassion for yourself, and by being willing to make a different choice because you understand why you feel a certain way and know you don't have to continue feeling that way.[3]

Choice is power, understanding is power, and we have that.

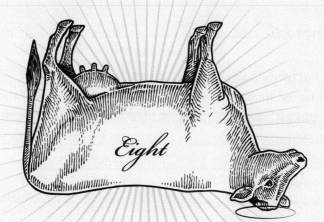

Living in Bliss and Other Myths

Bliss.

I love saying that word. It makes me feel sensual and sexy and light and filled with air. Just uttering that word brings to mind daydreams that involve long, slow touches that trail along the skin and a warm, relaxed afterglow. The word bliss, when it sits out there all by itself, makes me want chocolate, tequila, and sex. It makes me imagine biting into a truffle while making *mmm* sounds.

There is just something dreamy about the word bliss and the idea of living in it—think Ryan Gosling and Adam Levine working in your organic garden, both of them shirtless on a hot, sunny day while you bask in the warmth of the sun and the glow of their dreaminess, sitting on a chaise, drinking puckeringly tart iced limoncello, and sucking on a succulent strawberry freshly plucked from your bed of abundance. Now that's bliss, right?

Woe is me and rend some clothes, this is not, sadly, the case in my life. And if your life is anything like mine, you do not have Ryan and Adam in your backyard or anywhere else tending your real or metaphorical lady-garden either. Instead, you have Lego sets full of a zillion little rectangles that are too small for the adult human hand and bad directions full of pictures and arrows that wouldn't make sense to a genius. Okay, maybe a genius, but not this suburba-mom. Add in the dolls whose clothes cost more than your wardrobe, a dog who eats better than you do, oh, and that drink in your hand is a glass of Trader Joe's Two-Buck Chuck (which, by the way, is now two dollars and fifty cents! Is nothing sacred?). All of it, the Lego set, the doll clothes, the gourmet dog food, and the overpriced drink, really takes away from the dreamy bliss of your day.

Bliss equals perfect happiness, great joy. Yeah—like that's possible, if possible equals Armageddon.

Can I really live in bliss? I've got bills to pay, so bliss just doesn't seem to be on my radar. My love life is good, but after so many failed relationships, I'm good with dinner at Applebee's and a box of cream chocolates from the corner store. My work is inspiring, but I'm not hanging at the Chateau Marmont with

Orlando Bloom talking about my next project. And my kids—
well, let's just say at this moment one of them probably has the
other in a chokehold, screaming, "I wish you were never born!"

Bliss? Perfection? Really? Seriously, I mean, when I hear
someone say, "I'm living my bliss," all doe eyed and breathless, I
think, *No, honey. You're living in denial, or you're so full of shit
I could smell you before you walked in the door.*

Ouch, right? That seems a bit harsh, but really. Have you met
anyone whose life is a perfect great joy, like 100 percent of the
time? Yeah, me neither. So is living in bliss a myth? Maybe it's a
tease, sort of like going into a store because of a huge "50 percent off" sign in the storefront only to be told that the sale
already ended, and they forgot to take the signs down. Damn, I
hate that.

But living in bliss, or living your bliss, is supposed to be
glorious; it has to be, what with everyone trying to do it. Something to strive for, for sure. Like toned abs and buns. Or
climbing to the top of Kilimanjaro.

Again, I wonder, why am I torturing myself? Is the outcome
worth the work? And is it a maintainable type of thing? I would
say that most people come in and out of their toned abs (if they
have them), and we usually only climb anything once (if at all).
Why have I put on this expectation that I should be blissful?
More important, I wonder if there is anyone I can blame in particular for making this bliss thing *the* thing that everyone wants.
Besides Oprah.

The etymology of the idea of bliss can be traced all the
way back to the Sanskrit word *ānanda—ā* meaning all sides,
and *nanda* meaning pure joy. So bliss is joy from all sides. In

Hinduism, in order to reach Brahman (being conscious bliss, the highest reality) you'd have to connect all three dots, *sat* (truth), *cit* (consciousness), and *ānanda* (pure bliss) and then you would be totally connected from all sides to God.

But in order to do this, according to many a modern bliss expert as they quote the many ancient bliss experts, you must be completely devoid of attachments, anything that screams or whispers external sensory input. Which just seems really unrealistic. Perhaps for you, the idea of complete connection 24/7 to your higher source is possible, and for my part, maybe I'd have liked to be completely detached from all external sensory input, say, after my son had his first "food poop." But a great deal of the time, actually most of the time, I kind of like the sensory input. I've decided that this is okay. The trick is how we use that sensory input and what we understand bliss to be within the context of our lives.

The idea of bliss became popular as a modern Western concept because of Joseph Campbell. His idea was to follow your bliss, and thanks to PBS, which aired *Joseph Campbell and the Power of Myth* and his other shows over and over again for decades on end, many people glommed on. Next thing you knew, there were a whole bunch of bliss advocates telling you to get you some. And you should. Get you some, that is. It's just about being real about what your bliss is, not what gives you bliss. By this, I mean the difference between the soul's desire and earthly delights, because there is bliss and then there is sexy, fun, exciting, adventurous bliss—not that this is bad or anything, you just probably shouldn't design your whole life around getting it. I mean, look what happened to ancient Rome when everyone there decided to overdose on a truly mind-boggling level of hedonism. The city burned, supposedly while the Romans were still getting their delights on.

Joseph Campbell posits in *The Power of Myth* that if you follow your bliss, your true obsession in life, you will be in service to humanity to the highest possible extent. Now this seems somewhat doable between the driving the kids to sleepovers and the grocery shopping.

This Campbellian idea is also more about the self and less about becoming a no-self. So it's okay to maybe be a bit selfish here (because sometimes being selfish is actually a good thing, if you're being selfish in a non-selfish "I want to find my true bliss so I can live my obsession and in turn be of service to the world" kind of way).

This means that, alas, bliss is not about having Ryan Gosling as your lawn boy (okay, if I have to) and bliss is not about living your perfect obsession. As I said, bliss is akin to your soul's desire, and sensory pleasure often feeds into our emotional needs, and as Joe Campbell says for me to paraphrase, don't get stuck in your pleasure center, or decide following your bliss is a shopping spree at Nordie's or awesome sex.[1] It's probably true that sex with Ryan Gosling in the fitting room at Nordie's is blissful, but it's not your soul's desire, and it's most likely going to last about fifteen minutes and leave you feeling a bit empty a few hours later. Quick fixes usually have a way of doing that.

Why isn't pleasure bliss? I mean it can be, if you've done the work to ferret out what is real pleasure and what is pleasure based on the frenzied feeding of your emotional addictions and beliefs.

I love sex—I mean, really, who doesn't? But sex has *really* always been a pleasure spot for me. Growing up insecure and feeling unworthy of love, I decided if someone had sex with me, they loved me. In my twenties I had a lot of sex and a lot of broken hearts. I felt immediate pleasure and was filled with love, and then a few hours later, alone in my own bed, sadness would come. Instead of dealing with the beliefs about myself that put me alone in bed feeling sad, I would head right back out to feed the pleasure center again with shopping, food, and more men. Obviously I wasn't looking for or finding what my true bliss was (I have to congratulate myself here that I made it out of my twenties without a venereal disease or a drug addiction; even if I was after utterly pointless pleasure, I managed to be smart about it).

Every relationship I had was based purely on sex, right up to and including my ex-husband, because I had confused pleasure with bliss, sex with love, clothes with self-esteem, and . . . you get it. I didn't understand what bliss really meant, so I just went with what felt good at the time. Sure, that might be "living in the moment," but without an inner compass or at least an understanding of what my true bliss was, it was usually just a recipe for disaster. There's being in the moment and fully experiencing life consciously, and then there's being in a moment of sheer fear and survival, grasping at ropes you've measured the length of and anchored yourself to, only to find that they are not long enough or secure enough to get you safely to where you need to be.

After all my broken hearts, after all my letdowns and failures because I was looking for bliss in pleasure, I've finally realized bliss is my passion, and passion is my soul's desire (thanks, Joe).

I began digging deep to find my true soul's desire and spent less time putting a Band-Aid over my insecurities. Now, I look for what it is that makes me feel good, a type of good where I don't even realize I'm feeling good. You usually only see these moments in retrospect, because if you are in one, you are really in it. You're not thinking about how you feel. Instead, you're all the way taken up by the actual *feeling* of it. When you look at such moments, they are, in the truest sense, simply wonderful.

Every year my kids and I go camping. Especially after moving from the country to the big city, this reconnection with nature became even more important to us. This particular trip would be our first without their dad. It was all me and my mom, and the thought of putting up a tent alone did not thrill me. I found a place online that rented out cabins and yurts and even a teepee—and I thought, teepee? Perfect.

Before our trip we made American Indian costumes with feathers and paintings made on fake suede. Our excitement built as the day approached to embark on our Indian adventure. The drive wasn't long, about two hours, and all the way there we dreamed up our Indian life, our names, and our tribe. I, of course, was the chief, Princess Sky Dance, Elora was Princess Wild Flower, and Max was Indian Joe (a basic, salt of the earth name; that's my boy. He also had a total fascination with the name Joe, so we went with it—in retrospect maybe he was channeling his inner Joseph Campbell—ha, now that would be funny). We arrived at our teepee, and to our utter delight it wasn't some Disneyesque teepee designed for the modern traveler. It did have a floor, which I appreciated, but it was a full-on teepee with a glyph of a big bear painted on the side.

My kids leapt from the car, all dressed in their American Indian garb, and ran a full circle around our teepee. I was standing on the landing watching them, and as they made their way from around back to the front, they ran to me and at the same time leapt at me, arms wide open, eyes filled with wonder, and voices filled with pure love and joy. In that moment I felt pure bliss. It was one of the first moments my little family felt whole after my divorce, and it was one of the first times in a long time we all felt pure joy and excitement in the moment.

That's how I see that moment when I look back. When it was happening, I lost track of time and felt so much larger and smaller than I was, I was indiscernible from the experience. It was good. Good, as in "I lost track of time and space" good—it was bliss.

Bliss can be found in surprising places, like when something doesn't work out the way you expected, but you can look back and see that it was amazing, and you are smiling even as you think about it. That's bliss. Those are true enlightened experiences, and you'll know them because they don't fade away into a dark pit of realization that they're over. They linger for days as you continue onward, forward, and into your real bliss. And when you are following that bliss, you are in a way creating perfection, because you are being in the moment, consciously living the experience fully and thus not necessarily aware of the self. In that moment, you are experiencing ānanda. Connected on all sides to the experience of life.

As I became acquainted with the internal-monologue voices that always seemed to be talking at me in my head, I met one that always seemed to speak the truth. That voice would often remind me as I signed the credit card slip that this wasn't it. These shoes would not fill me, and I would be right back at that store again, sooner than I thought. And that's how I started to wonder, if this wasn't it, if he wasn't it, if the car wasn't it, what was it that would bring me true joy and fulfillment?

What was it that I truly loved to do, and had I ever actually felt bliss in my doing-ness before? It made me evaluate my shit. It made me decide to see what would happen if instead of meeting that guy, I wrote or read or spent time with my kids in a fully present way. And I began to be able to feel the difference, instead of just understanding it intellectually. I mean, we can all sit around and tell ourselves what we should do, but the minute we add a should, we rebel and our body takes over and that craving sends us right to that freezer filled with all the things we think will fill us but ultimately leave us wanting more. This new feeling of connecting with my soul's desire, my true bliss, filled me up. And that twinge of hunger, that thing that could convince me that I was starving, became silent in the face of my bliss-full self.

Have you ever recognized bliss? Some people haven't, which is probably one of the saddest things to think about. We rarely ask ourselves to remember, to think about the last time we felt absolute perfection. Why we don't ask ourselves, I can't say, but it's a worthwhile question, so here it goes: when was the last time you felt absolute perfection? I have an image of a teepee and my children's smiles that flashes in my mind when I ask that question. Other images follow, but that is where I go first.

This is how we figure out what our bliss is. We start by remembering what it felt like to be in that place of absolute goodness, overbrimming with all of that moment, full and replete in the essence of joy. We say, *That was bliss*. And hold it fast. We remind ourselves that it is different from Ryan-Gosling-in-the-backyard bliss.

As I began to examine my life, I realized that even amid the random nights with the guys I can't remember and the shopping sprees that ended with clothes I never wore, there were parts of my life that were blissful. And because I finally got that simple realization, I felt a new sense of gratitude for my parents, who always told me to do what I loved and that everything I needed would come. I wish I had been able to hear it earlier, but I was too young, and that bit of wisdom given to the young Betsy fell on deaf ears. But not now. Now I hear it and am empowered to do it (the day I finally got it, what my parents had told me, that moment was a bliss moment).

In retrospect, I can totally see where I stepped wrong, where I went off the bliss path. It was when I began to tie my bliss to my beliefs and my attachments to material things, and just like that, I lost it. Oh, what a tangled web we weave, right? But chances are if you look hard enough you'll find that there are actually pieces of your life that do bring you bliss; you've just overloaded your travel donkey with so much baggage, all you can see is the ass.

My bliss is creating art through music, movies, and writing. I found my bliss at age three when my father handed me a violin and said, "Do you want to play this?" My father was a musician and a teacher, and I loved watching him play. I would go with him to concerts and gigs, and I could read music before I could read words. That was a magical time. I could close my eyes and hear each of the instruments, and it moved me in a way I didn't quite understand. Time disappeared into the music, and I just was. So when he asked me if I wanted to play a violin, I said yes and off we went.

I had a natural talent for playing the violin, and I let it fill me because I didn't yet know to fear such things as my own talent. That fearless talent eventually won awards, played in orchestras, and once even played at the Hollywood Bowl. And being fearless, as children often are, I started twirling a baton around the same time (because when someone thinks about playing the violin, baton twirling naturally comes to mind), and at the age of seven I actually became a champion baton twirler. The pinnacle of my childhood bliss was finding my way into acting.

Success came easy because I loved it. I loved being on stage and using my imagination, I loved working with directors, and I loved the sound of a perfect minuet, but what I got caught up with was my beliefs about why I needed to do this. Somewhere along the way I lost the bliss, and I went from acting to being a professional child actor, and the work literally became life or death in my mind. Suddenly, becoming the best was more important than enjoying the process. And getting the part became vital because if I didn't, I believed my family wouldn't eat—or worse, I wouldn't be loved anymore. In my mind, my greatest value was in what I could do, not who I was. But it was more than that, because my ego loved being the best, loved the awards and the accolades and the love that was showered on me each time I won a new part. And my ego wanted to protect me from feeling unloved, so it pushed me to continue winning, even though none of it was my bliss anymore.

I forgot what I loved; I forgot why I had started doing the things I loved. Playing the perfect concerto on my violin became more important, not because of the joy it brought me to play—the feeling of the strings on my fingers, the warm vibration I felt through my body as the instrument responded to my bow strokes, the feeling of perfect control that I had of the sound. No, it became important because if I failed, my emotional addictions wouldn't get fed, my ego wouldn't get fed, my beliefs about myself would falter, and I'd be lost and alone.

Good-bye bliss.

By fifteen I had quit playing music, quit acting, and quit just about everything I loved, not because I didn't love it anymore but because I had lost the bliss of doing it.

Over time, I found my way back to something I loved by spending some time examining my life and what I wanted to do with it. It was a very spiritual thing without me realizing it was spiritual (as a side note, beyond some of the esoteric stuff like past-life regression therapy or communing with dolphins, a lot of this spiritual stuff is just common sense—we just seem to have lost it). I realized that maybe I wouldn't be an actress anymore. But I loved making movies and I loved the creative process, so when I was eighteen and I was asked to work on a really, really, really low-budget film about a bunch of hot girls romping around in the woods as CIA agents, I said yes. Working behind the camera came naturally; I had fun and thus began my illustrious career behind the camera.

For almost ten years I lived and worked happily in the entertainment biz. I climbed (I should say clawed) up the ladder from lowly production assistant all the way up to producer. I was successful, I made great money, and I had lots of friends. Until one day, right at the moment when all of my hard work was about to pay off, I got this strange feeling in my gut, a sadness as if I had lost something. The payoff, by the way, was a job offer at a studio, a job offer that, had I taken it, would potentially have landed me as a CEO of a studio one day. It was a path I had strived for all of my twenties, and at the age of twenty-six, my dream, my bliss was staring me right in the face, and all I could do was say no. What the fuck? No! Six figures a year, an office with a window, and a parking space—a key to the cool people's club—and I said no!

Perhaps it was that I felt I had hit bottom, creatively speaking. My creative bottom was slapped, as it were, when I produced a soft-core porn film. (Yes, ladies and gents, I produced soft-core porn and, to let it all hang out—nudge-nudge, wink-wink—and be my honest, authentic self, I've even produced porn-porn when times were slow. A girl's got to earn a living.)

Anyway, on this particular shoot, the director had a bit of a problem standing up, which went with his drinking problem, and literally fell over and passed out, which left me in charge of completing the scene at hand. The plot, and I use the term both loosely and ironically, involved two alien girls, scripted as Alien Number One and Alien Number Two, respectively, landing on earth with a mission to seek out mates so they could reproduce. The set was a bed on a platform, and the aliens were dressed in metallic, skin-tight, spandex unitards with large portions artfully cut away and black, thigh-high boots with six-inch heels.

But wait, it gets better.

After a brief look at the sketchy scene notes and a quick conference with the camera and sound guys, I turned to the girls and, with a staunch we-can-do-this tone, gave them their staging direction. Staging was, in fact, all I had to give them because there were no lines—that would have required some kind of actual plot. So I staged them and said, "Kiss her cheek," and watched, with ever-widening eyes, as Alien Number One promptly bent over while Alien Number Two kissed her ass. Immediately, and without thought, I said, "No, no—her *other* cheek!" Slapstick comedy ensued, of the "Who's on first?" variety.

There were other, less hilarious hijinks that led me to say no to the job at the top of the rung. They were little things, like losing passion for and interest in the films I was working on and instead working out of fear that I would one day not get hired. Eventually, all my experience led me to work for a company not doing soft-core porn, but it still wasn't really about creativity— it was about what sells. And with every film, I felt I sold a little bit of my soul and slid deeper and deeper into the business of films instead of the fun of filmmaking.

In hindsight, I know that it was my heart and my soul saying no, because once again I had tied my bliss up with the pleasure I had from the feel-good high I got from acceptance and success, which really was about my need to feel worthy. I've also noticed from my hindsight-studying that when I get stuck in pleasure mode, when I get stuck feeding the beast instead of the soul, life has a way of self-destructing on me. It's inevitable because constant pleasure has a way of turning into misery. I was making pretty good money while I was selling my soul, and life was pretty fun and easy and that can become very addictive, especially when suddenly I had money to buy what I didn't think I could get any other way.

Unless you are aware of what it is that truly brings you bliss and are willing to forgo the shopping spree, you'll always end up in debt. I loved making movies, and I loved the creativity, but the truth was I didn't want a desk job—which was what that big dream job meant. I was afraid it would expedite my slow slide from filmmaking to film business. Plus, I hated wearing suits. They just don't make women's suits for girls who are five foot two.

I liked wearing tennis shoes or boots. I liked that it was okay to show up to work not having showered because it was likely nobody else had. I loved never going to the same place twice. These were the things I loved about making movies. I loved the challenge of making something beautiful and creative on a shoestring budget, something that impacted people, and at that moment I was doing none of that. Amazing that I somehow heeded that voice in my gut, that even as I was blissfully unaware of my misery, I somehow knew I was miserable and made a choice that would eventually lead me back to bliss.

I instinctively knew it was time for a bliss reality check. I quit making movies and lost myself for a few years. Being twenty-six, no kids, and with a decent savings account, I played around for a while. I was still confusing pleasure with bliss, so eventually my bliss reality check ended up being tied up in a guy and thinking my bliss was marriage and the white picket fence.

As it turned out, the white picket fence was not my bliss, nor was the marriage or the guy. I found this out at the same time I found out that the guy had been cheating on me and really only cared about my BMW. I über found out he wasn't a part of my bliss when I went broke as I participated in the great American tradition of trying to buy my happiness and he was out the door and on to the next. It was when I was broke and brokenhearted that *Bleep* came into my life. And, like before, it was the simple act of having acquired more wisdom through life experiences and life openings that brought me to my bliss again, my obsession, my soul's purpose.

But nothing is forever and life often requires a tune-up. For ten years I lived that bliss until I woke to find it lost again. And once again I began picking up the pieces of my bliss, strewn about the reality I had created around it.

At the risk of sounding cliché, life is a constant reimagining and reworking, and we are always evolving and changing. Often we take the wrong off-ramp and have to backtrack a bit to regain our bearings. Bliss is something at my core; it's not walking around all doe eyed and full of love and light. Bliss is mostly messy. It's slippery and slides through my fingers and falls in between the cracks of life, but it's always there.

After living for forty-three years and having lost this bliss thing more times that I'd like to admit, I promise myself that this time, when I find it, I will cherish it, and I won't squander it. I won't take advantage of it, because what I figured out is that my bliss has never actually left me—I have left it. With each incarnation I experienced in my life—child prodigy, budding producer, author, and especially mom—my bliss was there hidden underneath the diapers and the dog poop. I just needed to see it, take it out every now and then, and say, "Hey, I remember you."

I have been following my bliss because my bliss is my life. Bliss, like happiness, love, and all those things we chase after, is right here within us. All we have to do is look for it.

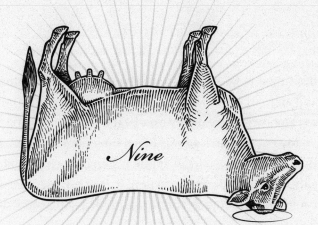

Nine

So, What Are You Wearing to the Masquerade Ball Called Life?

If I were invited to a dinner party with my characters, I wouldn't show up.

—Dr. Seuss, *The Sneetches*

The reality is most of us don't actually "know" anyone. How can we if we don't even "know" ourselves? Upon waking up the morning I knew I was getting a divorce, it became clear to me that I didn't know the man I called my husband. I only knew the character I had created for him, a character that fulfilled the character I had created for myself. Because ultimately all relationships are interactions with the characters we create, bouncing off each other like pinballs in an arcade game. We each play our roles diligently until one of us tires of that game, desiring a new costume or a new face, while the other is hurt and angered at our absolute gall to change costumes midstream.

And then the real fireworks begin.

My entire marriage was based on a figment of my imagination, a fairy tale told to me that I manufactured into reality, although based purely on fiction. Part of my fairy tale was that I could not love myself and that I needed someone else to do it for me.

In the beginning he was my knight clad in shining armor, sexy and smart, and an awesome lay. I was a beautiful young princess, powerful but feminine, and in need of a man who would whisk me off my feet, throw me on the back of his horse, and gallop away into the sunset. Even as the chinks in the armor began to show, I held on to my story because it was the only thing I believed would finally end the hurt hidden deep down inside. I certainly couldn't fix it. I either didn't know what needed to be fixed or was unwilling to do what it took to fix it.

I   I   I

I remember the night we met. I was new in town, a small town where word of fresh meat traveled fast. I was at the home of one of my fellow filmmakers, working on a new film, the news of which had also spread about town. I was the new girl who had landed smack dab in the middle of the cool people and, without realizing it, wore a big target on my back for all the "knights." I was the prize to be won, mounted, and eventually thrown out, used and discarded, when new meat came to town.

I realize now that I put that target on my back, as it fit nicely with my beliefs about myself at the time: damaged, suspended while moving, and not enough. I feel so much compassion for that younger self, and when I look back I want to give her a hug and say you are awesome and I value you. But without the learning of these early lessons I wouldn't be the me I am, so there you are. And there I was, the new girl, surrounded by people I thought knew more than me, trying to fit in, trying to feel relevant.

And the scene was set. Me, tipsy on the giddy feeling of being surrounded by all of these seemingly It People, and the It Boys knowing I was giddy, and him arriving on his horse (or sporty black Honda). Me, having just fallen off the back of another horse, I needed to be shown love, and I felt lost and insecure in a new place with no one I knew around. Because I was unable to show myself love, I looked outwardly for a man to do it for me. I attempted to fulfill my need to feel safe in this den of lions. I quickly donned my mask of damsel in distress, because that usually got the guy, and what I got was a romance novel complete with a Ryan Gosling impersonator, poetry gliding from his tongue and muscles gleaming. Cue the music and the sunrise, and off we went. What should I have expected, being an impersonator myself?

How does a relationship sour? How do we go from poetry and flowers and Sundays spent in bed to hate and resentment and fear and a bitter battle where everyone ends up bloody and headless? In retrospect, having taken the time to watch the replay with a broader understanding of why I made the choices I made, I believe it's because we fall in love with the mask, not the man, and we let the man fall in love with our mask instead of the real us.

As an actress, I played the role my husband wanted, the role I thought was the real me, the role I thought would make me happy. I played the role very well because I was so desperate for love and so afraid that no one would love me. I got so lost in the part, so method were my acting techniques, that I hid even the real me from myself.

To hide the shadows of our true selves, we create amazingly intricate masks designed to cover up the authentic face of who we are. The masks are created from the images of our beliefs about who we think others want us to be and the beliefs we carry about ourselves. They are carefully painted to hide what we so dislike about ourselves or are afraid to reveal, so pieces of us hide in the shadows, kept in the dark where even we often lose sight of them. Some dark part of me thought, *I am not really lovable, but if I wear this mask of worthy of love, then I will be loved*. So wear it I did.

I built my princess-and-supreme-hostess mask from the feathers of fear and rejection. I painted it with colors to ward off failure and everything I believed being vulnerable would bring me. I learned to gain what I wanted through other means, by wearing masks of my own creation.

In my marriage, before we had children and were free from the trappings of real life, kids, car payments, and laundry, it was easy to play the goddess, secure and happy and carefree; powerful, sexy, and smart. All the things my handsome prince wanted, and in turn he played gallant and brave, wise and all knowing, able to protect me from the dragons of the world.

Except that is not who we really were. Deep inside, underneath our masks of feathers, gold, and glitter were two maybe not completely broken but very dented individuals just wanting to feel loved and safe and secure and seriously hoping the other one would deliver that.

My relationship with my ex-husband was probably no different from most relationships out there. We started out madly in love—not with each other, but with an image we each projected outwardly. This was really hard for me to admit, this idea that I wasn't being authentically me, the reality that I had adopted certain behaviors in order to fulfill a destiny I thought I wanted, but hadn't really done the work necessary to make sure it was me that wanted it. It was terrifying and humiliating at first to say that everything I thought I was, I wasn't. I wanted to be the supreme hostess in a way, but I realized I didn't want it the way I had achieved it. By pretending and lying, I felt as if I had cheated myself because that reality wasn't based on anything but false beliefs and judgments. Was I creating this life out of fear or out of my true soul's desire? What did being happy and secure in myself, feeling true love, really look like? This was the work I hadn't done, because I never understood I needed to, or how.

Clearly my marriage was built on a foundation of fear and lack of self-worth, and somewhere along the line my ex-husband and I began to see the real people behind the masks. Even the best of actors break character every now and then, and every once in a while our soul's desire peeks out, like a glitch in the hologram. And it makes us wonder if that way is really possible. When finally I could no longer ignore the quirks in the system, I realized there were bugs I needed to weed out.

Even if you don't know it, the real you is within you. Even if you have covered it with so many layers it's impossible to see, it's there and working very hard to break free. My life after my divorce has been about finding that real me mixed in with all the masks I created. My process has been about uncovering the beliefs I have about myself and tearing down the reality I manufactured to hide those beliefs.

The whole concept of creating masks to hide who we really are is complex. Of course it is, because if we humans were easy, there would be no suffering, starvation, war, or general unhappiness. But hopefully the dots will be connected enough for you to find your way back to who you really are.

Ever since I was young, I believed I wouldn't be loved unless I was successful at whatever it was I was doing, be it acting, music, or business. I tied my self-worth to being perfect and exuding happiness. So outwardly, I wore the mask of a confident, sexy, secure, ballbusting woman, and in turn people loved me. And I believed they would never love me if I wasn't those things. We start out our lives as pretty, happy little beings, all warm and cozy in our Bugaboos, but slowly we gather up beliefs about ourselves and the world and how it works. And we start to worry that if we actually told other people about those beliefs, they might think we were seriously nuts, so we hide them. Sometimes those beliefs frighten us so much we hide them even from ourselves. Me, insecure and afraid of failure? No, not me!

We build intricate masks so we can fit into society and base them on what we think our communities and our family and friends want from us. We use them to hide our crazy, and we start to congregate around other people who wear the same masks. There is safety in numbers, or you could say like attracts like. But however you want to put it, we feel better when people agree with us.

Why did we become such good liars? If you think about it, it's no secret that our society doesn't really want to know the real us. At work, a woman showing vulnerability is often considered not up to the task of getting things done, so women put on the mask of emotionless robot or bitch. If a soldier were to tell someone he's conflicted about war, he would be considered weak, or a pacifist, so he dons the mask of coldhearted killer.

We think nobody wants to hear about it, so we cover up. What would happen if we let it all hang out, zits, stretch marks, and all? For a long time I worried that letting it all hang out would lead me into total seclusion and loneliness. No one would love me, and I would die alone. So, with my warrior mask securely in place, I moved forward in life, my eyes covered with feathers.

Imagine what would happen if, after your coworker asked you, "Hey, how's it going?" you said, "You know, my life kind of sucks right now," instead of donning the mask of perfection and saying, "I'm great!" Okay, perhaps some discernment is in order, and maybe dumping on your coworker right before the big staff meeting isn't such a great idea. But what would happen if you were honest, if you didn't try to hide your true self?

This has been an eye-opening exercise for me, this willingness to be real with people. Okay, I didn't just all of a sudden start running around playing the victim and complaining about how shitty I felt because my life was a mess, my marriage was over, and I was broke and lost and everything else. Instead, I started by playing with what was lurking in the shadows of myself. I began to bring those things out and express them openly. In that moment, they were the real me. Although they weren't pretty, if I wanted to find the real me underneath all the manure I had piled on top, I had to be the me I was at that moment. Only then could I expand, change, or become something else.

The real me at the time I got divorced, who was sweating and suffocating under the mask of flawlessness, was insecure. The real me was unhappy with my body, my career, and my marriage and unable to accept love, especially from myself. In that moment, that was real, but it didn't have to stay that way. To the shock of many of my friends and family, I began to show the chinks in my armor. I cried when for years I hadn't. When someone I knew asked me how I was, I told them, "I am in a very dark place," as opposed to putting on my pretty, happy, dancing mask. When I truly shared myself, others began to share themselves truly with me, and I suddenly realized I wasn't alone. I gained more friends than I'd had in a while, only this time I was being surrounded by people who also wanted to be authentically themselves.

At this point you might be wondering what this has to do with spirituality and living a spiritual life. Remember, I come from the belief that life—all of it—is spiritual, and peeling back the layers of the onion I've closed around my true self is the journey, the spiritual path. In doing this, I get closer and closer to my true self, my light self, my spiritual self, if you will. I decided that in order to become what I wanted, I needed to be who I was. I could undo what needed to be undone and find what had been underneath all along.

There was a balance here that I couldn't overlook. There was a risk of becoming a victim when I was doing this work of being my authentic self. Still, I had to continue to work on finding who it was I wanted to be, because I didn't want to swing the pendulum the other way. That would mean falling backward, back to sleep, only this time I might get stuck in the shadow world.

I began to find things in my life that reflected my true self, the self I wanted to be. My ex-husband had said I was mean, and that I wasn't compassionate, and part of me believed him. It stung when he said that, but once I took a moment to see beyond his reflection, I could see that I was actually a very compassionate being. I asked myself why I believed him. It all boiled down to "a winner never quits, and a quitter never wins," a saying engraved on a bracelet given to me by my father, whom I revered and adored.

Now, what I understand this sentence to mean now and what I decided it meant when I was six are two different things. Not entirely different, just nuanced. In my childhood home there was no room for complaining. My parents were of the generation that said you didn't complain about it, you just endured it, or if you could, you changed it. My father told me that if you wanted something you had to work for it. It probably wouldn't come easy, so if you wasted your time complaining and not working, you weren't going to get it. When he said this, his intention was to give me resilience, but I, in my limited understanding, took it to a whole new level where it has stayed for my entire life.

Somehow, my belief that winning would bring me love got twisted up with my father's words, and I decided that complaining was bad and would interfere with me getting the love I wanted. I was competitive from an early age—baton twirling, violin playing, dancing, singing, you name it—and I spent hours a day practicing. While other kids were out playing, I was in the driveway doing triple spins with my baton until I could no longer see out of my swollen eye (having whacked myself in the eye one time too many). Now you might think that my parents were awful for making me do all these things, but they weren't awful at all. My mother often begged me to come inside and even refused to allow me to practice into the wee hours of the night. I had taken on the belief that if I gave in—if I complained or even uttered a word about my exhaustion, my frustration, or my fear that I would never get it—I would lose all hope of achieving success. I was committed, and my parents simply honored that. Hence the mask of the warrior; I've got it all under control, girl.

Flash forward into my adult years. My mask securely in place, I often took others' (especially my ex-husband's) need to feel heard, whether about why they were upset or why their body hurt, as complaining. And I would offer a way to change it. That was my version of being compassionate. I believed that they really wanted whatever it was they were working on, or practicing, or desiring, and in my own little way, I was trying to help them. But in doing so, I lost sight of the possibility that they simply needed a moment to complain. They needed a shoulder to cry on, not advice, not tough love.

They didn't want a bracelet to wear. After coming to this realization, I asked myself, How can I still be compassionate and supportive without being harsh? My answer was to take off my mask and listen to them, without inserting my own baggage, my own fear of feeling vulnerable, and experience their vulnerability, and in turn my own.

When we are real, real with ourselves and with others, we gain the ability to see the masks of others and reach behind them. And if we hold our own and others' realness with compassion, we give each other a haven for that safety we all so desperately seek. In that safety you find a willingness to expose yourself, masks become unnecessary, and the real you shines.

For me, I found a sort of balance in the ability to be okay with being multilayered. As I did the work of uncovering myself, I found that I wasn't just one thing—there were many aspects of me and I could be all of them. I could love each and every part of me, the happy It Girl, the vulnerable girl. Sometimes hanging out with my layered selves hurt, but these named layers were no longer caricatures, masks. They were me, all of me.

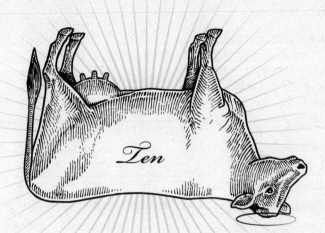

Ten

The Ego—the Monster in Our Closets

I have been sitting here for days writing this thing on ego over and over again, remembering all the little moments in my life that turned my friendly ego into a giant monster. After attempt number . . . well, I can't even remember, I finally realized that my ego wouldn't let me write this chapter. That's how big of a monster I have created. Writing this chapter requires me to remember stories from my past where I allowed my ego to rule to such a degree that I'm a little (probably a lot) embarrassed by it, embarrassed to expose the hidden truth my ego has worked so hard to hide.

I was a child actress, supporting my family. Well, not entirely—my parents worked, but they were both teachers and raising six kids, so yeah, my almost six-figure annual income helped. From the moment I was born, I was onstage—literally. I was a stand-in for a television news program doing a story about natural childbirth. The woman they had followed through her pregnancy ended up needing a C-section, so they just filmed my mom from the bottom end, and the rest is history.

Even my birth was a fraud. My arrival was filled with "lights, cameras, and action!" I was the star of the show, and that seemed to suit my ego just fine. So here I am, the child star and the baby of six kids. Just being the youngest can turn the ego into an insane monster, you know? Try adding cute, little, and very precocious, and shazam—ego baby!

I was a short kid, but I made up for it in confidence created by a constant feeding of my little baby ego. Since I had burdened myself with the responsibility of being the main supporter of my family (because I had created a belief about myself and success and love), I thought working was imperative to my—and their—survival. From the time I was eight, my ego, masquerading as the real me, could work a room. I could walk in and figure out in a minute what the producers wanted and deliver it. That's how it works in show biz, and I became a master at it. Never let them see you cry, and give them what they want; that was my motto.

Because I earned the major paycheck, I had a huge sense of entitlement. I was the ruler of the home roost, making sure everything revolved around me and that my wants and desires were catered to. I figured if I was going to get up at the crack of dawn to go smile for ten hours, I'd better have the prettiest room and the nicest clothes. I worked hard and felt I earned it. Forget that I had five older brothers and sisters all crammed into two smaller bedrooms at the other end of the house. And with every year and every success, my ego grew stronger—up until about age fifteen when being short and chubby cute but not the world's greatest actress stopped my career in its tracks. I still had my smile. But now, hiding deep underneath the shadow of my monster ego, were hurt and shame. Failure hadn't been an option, and in my little girl's mind I'd just failed—horribly. I just wasn't good enough, and that shame has lived with me my whole life.

Proving that failure wrong has driven my ego ever since.

Since I didn't have any money left to pay for college, and I didn't think I was worthy of it anyway, while all my friends went off to film school, my ego went into overdrive, scraping my way from the bottom of the ladder all the way to the top. It seems in this life I was born to have to work for it, and work hard I did. I went to work as a production assistant on films. By the time I was twenty-two, I had my own production company and was hiring as my production assistants a lot of those friends who had gone to college. The fact that I couldn't manage college and work at the same time left a chip on my shoulder.

In retrospect, I could have gone to college; I've often wondered why I chose not to. In uncovering the reasons why I made the choices I did in my life, I've come to see that my ego didn't want college because I was used to being the big fish in my little pond and my ego didn't want to compete with any other fish.

Plus, I had convinced myself that the only way I was going to succeed was the hard way, stubborn in my beliefs as I was. I spent every production meeting striving hard to be the brightest one in the room. I dated the guy who could make sure I was hired, even if my credentials didn't muster up to the job qualifications. When you're in charge, you get to hire who you want, and I often stacked the deck in my favor.

I am comfortable looking back on my old self now, because we've all been little shits in our lives in order to feed our ego, especially when that ego is what's protecting us from what we fear the most. Using my skills as an actress and a perceptive people reader, I managed to convince a lot of people a lot of the time that I knew what I was talking about. What I lacked in book smarts, I made up for in street smarts. There was no way my ego was going to take another beating with the failure stick.

I worked my way up to executive at a production company and weaseled my way into the corner office. Whatever it took, my ego did, armor on and ready for battle, my tongue like a sword even as I smiled coyly. I liked that people were afraid of me. I liked that I had a lot of friends. Never mind they were all in the biz and their friendship probably had something to do with the fact that I was the one employing more than four hundred people. My ego was happy and apparently that was all that mattered.

I was actually good at my job (at least I think I was). I kept rising toward the top. Somewhere deep inside was that soft little girl who just wanted to be loved, chosen, and appreciated. But having lost that once, I allowed my ego to create such fear of having it ever happen again that I built this incredible cage of steel around me that nothing could penetrate. Work and success were all that mattered.

Somewhere around age twenty-seven, when I was on the verge of being hired for a job that would have been a major advancement career-wise, I had the realization that something wasn't right. Nothing I could put my finger on. I just stopped enjoying my life. I realize now that I had lost my bliss and had replaced it with fear and doubt.

When you're unaware of your soul's desire and living happily in shoe consciousness, the soul will use anything available to send you a message. In my case it was literally my gut. But instead of diving into a deep exploration of self, I took some antacid, went shopping, and had an epiphany based on what I believed was what I really wanted. I've since learned that epiphanies based on the advice given in *Cosmopolitan* are probably not the ones you should jump into, Jimmy Choos first. Not entirely anyway. My gut was on to something, but I just used the same old tools I had used before to help me whittle myself a new life. I had no idea I was carrying around a set of beliefs that didn't fit, protected by an ego who just wanted to avoid being hurt again.

So I turned the position down, quit my job, quit Hollywood, and retreated into what I thought was a new life, which entailed starting a gourmet dog treat business with a guy I thought I loved but really was just having great sex with. A man who had no entrepreneurial spirit and really just dug my BMW and the fact that I was out of town a lot on business so he could take out other women in my BMW. When we carry around our bag of beliefs, every choice we make starts with something from that bag. Since I didn't understand that my bag was filled with low self-esteem and fear of being abandoned, my ego, my protector, told me to grab what I could, by force if necessary, and make it work.

I I I

It would take two years of flailing, failing, and crashing into an abyss before a life jacket called *Bleep* came along. Well, actually, it was called *Sacred Science* at the time, but it became *Bleep*.

Upon stepping into my newfound pasture of "new thought," one of the first things I was told was to get rid of the ego. Ego— okay, I kind of knew what that was, and usually when someone brought it up, it wasn't pretty.

In spiritual practices, the ego sacred cow is described as the part of us that makes this illusion real. It's said that reality isn't really real unless the ego says it is. It's the part of us that fights for our individuality; it creates order for us from the chaos of the world. It gives us the sense of being human and is apparently the main cause of all our woes, because the ego helps us hide from our true nature, our true self.

As the grounder, the protector of the reality we have bought into, the ego helps us design our outer shell, our masks, if you will, and from there we unconsciously feed it, over and over again. Our ego is tied to our emotional experiences, which could be a good thing if we have tipped over all of our other sacred cows and are living our true selves. Alas, our ego does get in the way because we're human, and once we like something, we want it over and over again, and when we don't like something, we avoid it like the plague, and our ego is sort of in charge of that.

The problem with our wonderful ego arises when we let it run roughshod over our true self, the one underneath all the beliefs and masks and sacred cows. So our ego is simply doing what it thinks it should be doing, running around like a self-pleasing monster, eating up all the chocolate cake it can find because we like it, it gives us pleasure, it makes us feel real when we eat the chocolate cake. Our ego is a winner-takes-all kind of girl. It's dead set on delivering what we want, and it will act accordingly to get it. But we aren't really telling the ego what we want—we're letting our beliefs do the talking.

As I child, I learned that success fed my ego. Failure hurt, so every time I got a role or won an award, my ego got fed, and every time I didn't, my ego went hungry. As I grew, my ego got creative in how I could feed it—more money, more success—because after a while just one piece of cake wouldn't do! As an adult, I worked in a man's world. Surrounded by men, I was short and cute; add that to being a woman, and it made it hard to succeed (this was hard for my ego to take and hard for my normal, thinking, feminist brain to take as well*).

Back to my point about my ego and what it thought. My ego figured if I wanted success, it was going to make me tough and rough and more like one of the guys. It helped me design a mask that would help me get that. And then my ego paraded around town, strutting its stuff for the world to see. For a while this worked just fine. It takes time for truth to seep down through all the cow manure we pile on top with the help of our ego, so sometimes it takes a while before the true self can be heard over the roar of the ego. But when it is finally heard, even if it's not totally understood, what was working usually stops working. So all my little tricks of the trade became inadequate to fill my empty heart. My skills as a producer, the newest designer shoes, the hottest men: none of it was enough to ease that sick feeling in my gut. My true self spoke to me through my body, because that was the only way I would hear it.

Here's the thing—the ego isn't inherently the bad guy. It's just trying to please us, it's saying, *Here, you want success? I'll give it to you, I'll make it real.* The bummer part of that is that because we have allowed our beliefs about who we are, what we want, and what we should do to take charge, well, it's sort of like letting your five-year-old pick what he wants for dinner—he's always going to go for dessert. So the ego gives me what I want. It protects my true feelings and stops my fear from being exposed to the world. It often hides my feelings and fears from even myself. That's how good our ego is at doing its job: most of the time we don't even know it exists, but we do know when it's been bruised.

❚　❚　❚

Being the stand-in baby was a perfect setup, a perfect metaphor (and you can tell how much I love a good metaphor) for my life right up to this moment. From the days of waiting in the casting director's lobby, hoping to be "the one" so I could please my parents, make money, and succeed, to waiting for that guy to call so I could feed my ego's need to be wanted and loved, my ego has never felt safe or been fully satiated. It's been on constant red alert and focused on covering up the beliefs and fears hidden behind it, because those fears were not going to get me what I wanted. Until I become conscious and aware of my true thoughts and emotions, until I clearly understand where they come from, the ego will continue to fight the battle for me. But it does have reinforcements. The true self (the voice of reason and love in our heads) is often soft-spoken, but if heeded, it can negotiate you out of even the fiercest of battles.

Ever since I plummeted into the world of "spirituality," I've heard people blame the ego for everything, but I've always felt a kind of disconnect when it comes to ego bashing. Thing is, it's a part of us. It's what helps us experience our humanness, and if we bash our ego, aren't we bashing, well, us? And we create it. Unconsciously maybe, but we create it. I guess it feels good to say, "I've let go of my ego." But isn't that just the ego congratulating itself for letting go? It seems like all this talk about the big, bad ego is just us letting our egos run over all the things we know about the ego. And ego doesn't find irony funny.

When I was twenty, after going to a self-help seminar called the Landmark Forum, I came out telling anyone who would listen about what an asshole I was. I was so proud to be able to say that. But admitting I am an asshole doesn't stop me from being an asshole, does it? Is it the ego admitting to being an asshole, or is that our true selves admitting to being an asshole? I'm going with the ego just grabbing on to the idea with a yippee! It is like ego-smack, running around bashing ourselves; it simultaneously shows that we know something and that we are self-aware and self-effacing.

How is a gal, then, supposed to separate herself from her ego? It's kind of like the earth and the moon, a package deal. It would probably be pretty sucky for good ol' planet earth if it didn't have the tidal pull of the moon and the moon's ability to take a meteor hit for the team now and again. If you think about it, that hanger-on has real purpose. Perhaps, thought I, ditto on la ego?

It seems silly, when given a nice earth-needs-moon-for-tidal-action-and-meteorite-shield metaphor, to throw my ego out like it's doing me wrong. Our ego isn't bad—it just needs a little management, some gravitational pull, if you will, to keep it on an even-keel path.

When we look at it straight on, it seems like sitting around bashing the ego that's "us" just makes us start to doubt ourselves even more. Judging our ego just makes us dislike ourselves—maybe even hate ourselves.

Wow! What a mess I've made taking the easy road, falling back and letting my ego do all the work instead of taking the time to be conscious of how I'm really acting. That's why my ego hasn't let me write this chapter 'til now. Because in doing so, it has been exposed. But don't worry, ego. I won't throw you out. I'm just going to put you under new management—*conscious* management.

My ego is a tool (duh, tool as in *tool*), here to help me succeed in being any sort of person I want to be. It is part of my human experience, an experience I want to live fully. I can use it as a barometer of my feelings, my true feelings, the ones I've uncovered underneath my masks and beliefs about myself. If I'm living and operating from my true self, my ego has no way of confusing what I really want. It's my soul's desire, and it's clear, and my ego can feed on that all day.

Note

* I would like to say, just briefly and because I have an opportunity here, that I have some disappointment that this uphill battle due to having a vagina and breasts is *still* pretty universal across the cultural board. What the hell, all the people of the world? It is sad to say that I can point out, without actual bias or hyperbole, that we chicks ended up with the suckiest challenge-mountain to climb from beginning to end. I mean, check out that grade—it has to be 90 percent or some shit. And while you're checking that out, check out the history of the world. We of the tribe Vagina do not end up being, or being treated as, Chief Grand Poobah very often. We are far more frequently treated like a non-queen of poo-poo. We've made some strides, but it's going to be a while before that tide turns ("binder full of women": I rest my case).

Eleven

Fear and Judgment,
the Real Battle for Survival

I hate to fly—I mean seriously, I hate it with the white-hot intensity of a thousand suns, I hate it so much. I am your worst nightmare on a plane; bless you if you end up sitting next to me. I sweat, I hyperventilate, and if you're game, I talk to you about anything. I am happy to chat about your last colonoscopy if that's all you got—whatever, bring it on, just don't let me think about being in a metal tube, rocketing through the sky at thirty thousand feet. It all seems so unnatural and pushes up against my need for control and my fear of free falling from thirty thousand feet. Since I'm so eager to chat, I've met some really interesting people on planes and had some pretty interesting talks about fears.

I once met a young man, gosh was he a cutie, setting off to Iraq. As he boarded the plane, I could instantly tell he was a soldier. He was with a bunch of other soldiers, all dressed in street clothes, but clearly freshly shaved and ready for battle. This one must have drawn the short straw because he ended up sitting next to me. He sat down, and I didn't even hesitate to launch into my sob story about my fear of flying. I said outright, "Listen, I hate to fly, so if you don't mind, I'll chat you up for an hour and half and be on my way." He laughed and said, "Sure."

I grilled him about his life, what he did in the military, and why on earth he had joined in the first place. This was all before takeoff. As the plane sped down the runway and the nose lifted into the air, I grabbed his hand, and you know what?—he held it back. If I weren't on a small plane, I swear I might have married him on the spot.

He was a perfect gentleman with a slight southern drawl and about nineteen, which put him into the cute and too young category, but this didn't stop me from having an hour-and-a-half-long love affair. He asked me what I did, and when I said I was a writer, he got this faraway look in his eye. He hesitated for a moment before he said, "I wanted to be a writer. I've been writing poetry since I could spell, and I always wanted to write a novel."

I am always amazed at the confessions we make to complete strangers, the freedom we feel to tell it like it is because the person we're confessing to will never tell anyone and probably doesn't care anyway. But I did. I asked him why he didn't become a writer, and this nineteen-year-old, southern Adonis (seriously, he was hot) looked at me and said, "I was afraid I would fail and my family and friends would be disappointed in me." So instead he joined the army and was heading into violence and physical danger and possible death, as if losing his life in a war was less frightening than being told his writing was bad.

Fear is the grand bovine of sacred cows; we don't even realize how sacred our fears have become, how protective we are of them, and how fiercely we will fight to hide them from the world. Our ego has worked overtime to hide them, creating masks that cover the beliefs that stem from our secret fears. Our nightmares are a bevy of these thought monsters that have been lurking in the recesses of our brains and come out from the shadows to torment us.

There is a moment in childhood when fear takes hold, usually about the time we realize that our parents are human and flawed, and we suddenly grasp that we too won't be perfect. We wonder to ourselves what our flaws will be. Soon enough they are shown to us through the actions of others. We grab hold of those hurts, and with the power of the imagination so carefully cultivated and encouraged by our grownups, we fabricate thought monsters out of the threads of words and comments hurled at us. These monsters will haunt us for our entire lives.

I distinctly remember the moment as a child when I realized my parents weren't all-knowing, all-powerful beings of perfection. The biggest contributor to this was when my father could not explain to me the rationale behind believing in an invisible

God who was hell-bent on killing me. My father, who, I believed, knew everything there was to know. My father, who knew instantaneously when I was lying, even when it seemed impossible for him to know. My father, who had an answer for every random "why" question my five-year-old self could muster, suddenly and shockingly admitted he didn't know something. In that instant, my world shattered. My father wasn't perfect. I also remember how for most of my young life I thought my mother was the epitome of beauty. I believed that she had nothing but love for herself until one day in a store dressing room when I heard her muttering in frustration about how she was short and nothing fit her. At that moment I thought, wait a minute, I'm short. Is this a bad thing?

No one likes to admit fear. We are taught early that being afraid is a weakness, especially our little boys, who grow up to think they should be our warriors. I went to a movie the other day with my five-year-old son, and as we watched a trailer for a big action movie, he grabbed my hand, and I held his back. He asked me, "Are you afraid, Mama?" I said, "Yes, it's scary." And he said, "That's because you are a girl." Hmm, I thought, where did he pick that up? Channeling my best Will Smith voice, I said: "If we are going to survive this, you realize that fear is not real. It is a product of thoughts you create. Now do not misunderstand me—danger is very real, but fear is a choice."[1]

Okay, I didn't really say that. But boy, isn't that the truth! I did say something like that, only more for a five-year-old and in a cute voice. I also told him that fear was an equal opportunity bandit and that boys can be as afraid as girls, and that true warriors will admit it, face it, and conquer it.

One of the greatest awakenings I've had recently was that the fear I had held onto the tightest, the fear of being abandoned and alone, had finally broken free. This is what happens when we lock away our fears instead of facing them as they come. Eventually, like a cyst festering for years, it bursts, and when it does, it's usually messy and gross.

My entire life I have feared being abandoned because I wasn't good enough. I worked hard to be the best at everything and to please everyone I could so they would love me. I put on the mask of warrior goddess and wore it well. I wielded a mighty sword so swift and piercing that people were afraid of my wrath. Outwardly I appeared strong and fearless, while inwardly I was a cowering child. The thought monsters I conjured were evil and menacing, and to cover up my fear, I judged others harshly for their weaknesses. I rarely cried, I never allowed myself to feel pain, and when it hurt so much I couldn't handle it, I lashed out uncontrollably. Then I hated myself even more for my weakness of feeling, hated that I was afraid of anything.

How often in your life have you avoided doing something because of the terrifying story you concocted in your head? Maybe you avoid flying or swimming in the ocean (amazing how the film *Jaws* forced many of us back onto the beach). Our brains are very convincing; we've learned to tell ourselves the story of fear so well. Our brains don't even know the difference between what's happening outside of us and the wild tales we've conceived all on our own. The brain lights up the same and the body reacts in tow as if it's "real." Once belief sets in and the habit is formed, our bodies be damned—they can't change it. I've lost count of how many times I have played out a scenario in my head and watched my body begin to sweat and my stomach tie up in knots. All because of a movie playing in my head that had nothing to do with reality.

And I can admit that sometimes I've gone ahead with the conjuring of the thought monsters even though I knew I was doing it. We begin to like our fears, and our ego steps up to hide them, protecting them like children so we don't have to face them and risk losing them. We begin to feel safe with our fears because our body is used to them. Isn't the definition of insanity doing the same thing over and over again while expecting different results? I mean, it's sort of absurd if you think about it. It defies logic, and yet we still do it over and over.

We humans with our wild imaginations can take a molehill and turn it into a mountain in a nanosecond. Hey, we like the chemicals our fears release, and there is no rational reason given to us to change something that seems to feel so good. Who stops something that feels good, right? I know damn well I am going to regret that second helping of ice cream, but I take it. We create clever ways of hiding our fears, and we give birth to a cacophony of voices that will reinforce all of the reasons why we should keep on hiding, why we should be afraid so we don't forget to. Soon, we become ruled by the peanut gallery in our head.

They are those little voices that egg you on as you head to the freezer to grab the caramel pecan ice cream for a three-scoop "snack," creating a masterful set of justifications as to why three scoops won't be bad—you're going to yoga class tomorrow, you need it, you're in a shitty mood, he didn't call, and why should he, you're not worth it anyway, of course you didn't get the job, you're not really good enough for it anyway, so go get the ice cream. It will make you feel better.

All the while there is another voice in our heads, the judge, and although we think it's on our side, it really isn't. The judge is sort of like the tongue of a serpent—lashing in and lashing out. Judging us and judging everything outside of us that doesn't fall into line.

We live one story on the inside and another on the outside. On the inside we just want that ice cream because we've told ourselves (with the help of the peanut gallery) it's the only thing that will make us feel better. Our judge stands back mocking us, calling out the cellulite on our thighs and the glaring fact that we couldn't get the job because we don't have a college degree.

That same judge is the first in line to judge others around you who might point out some of those fears you're so desperately trying to hide, a judge and jury all wrapped into one. Give them a quick wit and a sharp tongue and you're dangerous. The judge can call you out on your shit, but no one else can.

If you grew up with brothers and sisters, you'll remember how your siblings could punch you in the stomach at will. However, if anyone outside the family threatened you with a cold knuckle sandwich, your siblings were the first to jump in and squash that outsider like an ant on a picnic table. I can mess with my brother, but you can't. Yep, that's our judge.

Our fears tag on to our beliefs. No one will love me because I'm not worthy of love. Fear of being unloved begets an outward appearance of not needing love, which in turn sends a warning to the judge and jury in our heads to hand down a verdict on anyone or anything that dares raise a finger to confirm our own fears. Face it: it's a whole lot easier to judge others than to look at ourselves. And when we do finally look, the judge turns on us with a vengeance, reminding us why we are unworthy of love, so we decide rather quickly not to do that again. Like a child burned by a stove, we are scorched by the searing heat of the self-hatred we put upon ourselves.

This may seem over the top. You may be thinking, "I don't hate myself." Now, I'm nothing if not dramatic, but I can honestly admit to you that I have hated myself. After admitting that to others, I have found that many of us have felt that hatred at one point or another. Okay, so you don't have to admit hate, but ask yourself how tightly you hold on to your beliefs about right and wrong; ask yourself how often you judge those who don't agree with you or seem to have the ability to see right through you to where your fears are hiding. There is nothing more satisfying to our judge and jury than self-righteousness. I have become judgmental of people who don't have judgments against themselves, maybe because I want everyone to be like me. It will make me feel better . . . probably. But I'd be willing to bet that the loudest in the room to scream, "I love myself!" is probably lying.

Fear is a thought monster we conjured out of false beliefs we took on because we didn't know any better, and judgment is the weapon we use against ourselves and others to protect our fears.

▌ ▌ ▌

Fear was once used by our little brains as a survival mechanism, but we've just taken survival way too far. We've gone all mountain man on it and stored food and guns in preparation for the apocalypse. Seriously, people, 2012 came and went, and we're all still here! It's time to disarm and come down off the mountain. Danger, on the other hand, is real; it's why we have a fear button. But leave it to us humans to take a system perfect for saving us from, say, a real bear in the woods, and screw it up so that we're afraid even when the only bears around are the ones we've created. Because that is what we do. I have noticed in my own life how often I have not actually been present to what was being said, how often the words of others transmuted as they entered the world I had created in my head. The words become distorted and colored by my beliefs and the desire to be agreed with. I hold on to a desperate desire to be loved, but believe I won't be, so every word, every gesture of love, is tainted as it enters my mind. The thought monsters take over and whisper, reminding me that it is a lie, and like a good soldier, I follow my leader and self-destruct any opportunity for love. All the while my ego is saying, "See? You will never be loved. Now are you going to eat that ice cream or what?"

Why is it that so many of us feel we need crisis in order to face our fears, to bring about the change we already know we need to undertake? After my last big crisis, I asked myself this question. It seemed my crisis meter had an alarm clock and every ten years I brought about a doozy. Stubborn as I was, the complete annihilation of everything in my life was beyond the scope of what I thought I could manifest. But it was necessary, because in the aftermath, as I stood amidst the flames of my life, I saw that fear had been my leader. Even as I fought to keep it at bay, ultimately that is what brought me to this moment.

As I sat on that plane and listened to the young soldier (you remember, the soldier heading off to battle in Iraq) speak of his love of writing and how he had conquered his fear of death and was willing to enter the ultimate manifestation of humanity's collective fears and judgments of others while simultaneously carrying an internal fear that held court over his creative expression, I felt compelled to ask him if he had any of his writing with him. I already knew he did, and as expected, he reached into the small bag he had stowed under the seat and pulled out a small, ratty, black book.

He read me his poetry, his confessions, his deepest darkest fears, hidden underneath the bravery of his uniform. It was absolutely beautiful, profound, honest, and raw, and I cried and told him that he was indeed an amazing writer and that he had one fear left to conquer. It was a fear greater than the fear of battle, and the warriors on the other side would be mightier than any he would face in Iraq. He had to battle his own demons, his own beliefs about himself, and the programming so lovingly placed on him by people who didn't know any better. Because if he didn't do it now, he might never do it, his chance taken away in a distant place, thick with a different kind of fear.

Just like your beliefs and your masks, it's time to take stock of your fears and face them. Because if the Law of Attraction, that idea that we manifest our realities based on ideas and energy we project out onto our world, is all it's cracked up to be, then chances are you're going to create a reason to face your fears one way or another. It might as well be on your terms.

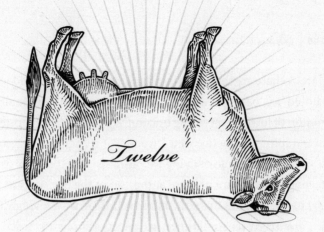

Twelve

Self-Love?

Be who you are and say what you feel because those who mind
don't matter and those who matter don't mind.

—Dr. Seuss

L ove yourself unconditionally. That's what almost every guru,
parent, and self-help book I've ever read tells me. But I wonder: do they really love themselves unconditionally? I myself
have uttered this absurd phrase to my own children, and often
they look back at me with a roll of their eyes. Yeah, right, Mom.
I'll do that when you do. Damn kids. How is it that they see right
through me? I mean, let's get real here, people. There are parts of
ourselves that we just don't "love unconditionally." There are
body parts, personality parts, family parts, men parts, women

167

parts—there are things we just don't *love* and why should we? Why should we be expected to *love* anything unconditionally? This notion of loving everything unconditionally is in the top-ten list of every spiritual practice. But I wonder if it's actually possible, or if it's just another rule of living we push on ourselves only to end up feeling like a failure because at the end of the day we can't achieve it. I'm happy to tip this cow, and I promise to do it lovingly.

The truth is, sometimes we set conditions in order to love something. Like, I love my boyfriend, but do I love him unconditionally? Nope, I have conditions, baby, and I expect him to love me for them! I love him for a lot of reasons, including his conditions on me, but if I'm really being honest, if I really look at why I am in this relationship, one of the big reasons I love him is because of how he makes me feel. I love that he makes me feel sexy, and I love it when he does something sweet or romantic and makes me feel beautiful and special. I love him because he laughs at my bad jokes, and I especially love him because he answers the phone late at night when I can't sleep and listens to me rant and rave about why I don't love myself—now that's love, and if he didn't, I probably wouldn't love him. I am always baffled by people who tell me that their relationships don't make them who they are. People who say, "I don't expect my (lover), (husband), (partner) to fulfill my need for love. I am complete and whole on my own. I provide all the love I need." Bullshit. Why are you in a relationship then? Why did you pop out of the love bubble of oneness with the universe and land in this reality and this body at all then? How can you be here if you're still enveloped in a circle of love all of the time? Why haven't you gone poof right back to the bubble of love you came from?

Perhaps I've spent too much time hanging out around the smoke circle, but I have genuinely had this conversation more times than I can count, and with each word of unconditional love uttered, I could smell the stench of cow manure. You might think I'm just cynical, and maybe I am a bit when it comes to love, but when pressed, these same masters of love often admitted that in fact there were pieces of them that meant they weren't the perfect box of chocolates, that there were, in fact, pieces they had taken bites of and just put back and ignored.

To those people who run around shouting about how much they love themselves, refusing to admit they've got a few bad pieces of chocolate in their boxes, come on! We've all got them, and you know what? That's okay. That's actually healthy, and it's authentic—at least to me.

What pressure we put on ourselves when we create this expectation that we must love ourselves unconditionally. Love ourselves or we won't truly love someone else, love ourselves or we'll never find true peace. If that's the height of the bar, then I'm doomed to live a lonely and unhappy existence way underneath it. Because the truth is, I don't always love myself unconditionally. Sometimes I am a total asshole, and I know it, and I don't love myself when I am that.

What does it mean to love unconditionally? What is love?

Have you ever looked up love in the dictionary? How interesting that one four-letter word can have so many meanings. There are at least thirteen different definitions of love—my favorite being a score in tennis, by the way. I also find it interesting that it's first listed as a noun, when often it feels like a verb or an adjective. But it can be considered all of the above, which seems sort of fitting for this particular word, don't you think?

For fun, here are the thirteen definitions of the word *love* that I found at Dictionary.com:

Love, *noun*, *verb*, **loved**, **lov·ing**

1. a profoundly tender, passionate affection for another person.
2. a feeling of warm personal attachment or deep affection, as for a parent, child, or friend.
3. sexual passion or desire.
4. a person toward whom love is felt; beloved person; sweetheart.
5. (used in direct address as a term of endearment, affection, or the like): *Would you like to see a movie, love?*
6. a love affair; an intensely amorous incident; amour. sexual intercourse; copulation.
7. (*initial capital letter*) a personification of sexual affection, as Eros or Cupid.
8. affectionate concern for the well-being of others: *the love of one's neighbor.*
9. strong predilection, enthusiasm, or liking for anything: *her love of books.*
10. the object or thing so liked: *The theater was her great love.*
11. the benevolent affection of God for His creatures, or the reverent affection due from them to God.
12. Chiefly tennis. a score of zero; nothing (now isn't that ironic?).
13. a word formerly used in communications to represent the letter *L*.

If we focus on the main emotional definitions of love, there are basically four: maternal, family, friendship, and romantic. I know I will always have love for my children (maternal love), even if I do sometimes fantasize about dropping them off at their grandma's and leaving with Ryan Gosling for an island far, far away (I jest, I jest!). To gain maternal love, all you need is one night of fun, nine months with no alcohol—which is probably a good thing because you may have ingested too much on the one night of fun anyway—and, in my case, forty-four hours of labor and a nice scar across your once bikini-ready belly. I'd better unconditionally love that little being, because I sure as hell ain't loving my belly anymore. Seriously, I do unconditionally love them. It's instinctual. Even if I tried not to, I probably couldn't.

The chemicals released and the part of the brain that lights up during maternal love is completely different from the part that lights up during friendship or romantic love. Love for friends and romantic love, now those babies have some conditions! Those two are tied to so many things. So many expectations and attachments to the past (conditions!). There are at least a dozen specific parts of the brain that are activated when we feel romantic love, which leads to a release of all sorts of yummy pep-tides. These peptides influence certain behaviors ranging from pleasure to sadness (seriously, just read a book on neuroscience if you want the gory details; if not, just take my word for it that this is how your brain works).

So our brain and the chemicals produced in our body work with us for romantic love and maternal love. One setup without conditions and the others with a whole lot of conditions. I suppose there are even conditions in tennis, but since I don't play it, luckily I won't have to tackle that type of love! But what about self-love—what about this idea that we must unconditionally love everything? Where does that fit into our brain?

Unconditional love is often expressed as having no bounds and being unchanging. When it comes to the people, places, and things in our lives, that is just unrealistic, unless of course you live in utter denial of your humanity and without any expectations or attachments. Seriously, you're a zombie at that point. That is not actually living, so you might as well polish your spaceship and take off.

The idea that we should (oh, I love that word—should. Ha!) walk around "allowing" everything and everybody to be whatever they choose and that we should just "love them unconditionally" is tantamount to having a frontal lobotomy. Sometimes I see that the nuances in life get lost in our desire to be the perfect picture of spiritual beings. Sometimes the idea of love gets confused with the notion that love means being a doormat, or being, well, lovey-dovey, ooey-gooey, warm and fuzzy. But what if love is sometimes the opposite? Is it possible that loving unconditionally means being tough and hard and strong? The answer, of course, is yes.

I am often the evil witch of a mother because I say no. The audacity! No, you cannot eat cupcakes for dinner; no, you cannot wear your bathing suit to school; no, you cannot go on the roof with me to hang Christmas lights, even if you are wearing your bicycle helmet. All parents know that sometimes saying no is the greatest sign of love there is.

We all know that sometimes loving another person means not giving in to their behaviors because we know that their behaviors probably won't help them in the long run. Like with a drug addict, we offer compassion instead of just giving them what they want, no matter how hard they pull at our heartstrings.

In our relationships we are compassionate and understanding, but usually we are willing to walk away when our conditions aren't met. It may take a while, years even, but eventually most of us move on. Even though we may still care for the other person, love them unconditionally, we do not. Except Ryan Gosling—I think I do love him unconditionally.

We can be quite rational about this with everything except ourselves. We either beat ourselves up over our failures and feel no love or compassion, or we hide behind a false sense of bravado, advertising our love for ourselves via our social media accounts. I am guilty of posting great quotes about self-love while secretly loathing myself.

Here's the trick, the distinction I've finally come to after years of shoving the cotton-candy concept of loving myself down my throat: it's not about love at all—it's about compassion. It's about forgiveness and acceptance. Maybe it's just easier for us to call it love, but I didn't see the words *compassion* or *acceptance* or a warm and fuzzy celebration of one's large hips in any of those definitions. In my life right now, I am interested in being real about what these words mean and what I really need in order to find peace or love of self, if that's possible (don't worry; it is).

This became clear to me during my divorce. Divorce is almost never pretty, and it's usually the time when the worst in you comes out. It was no different for either me or my ex. It's that mask thing, you know, the ones we wear so people won't know the real us? When my ex-husband and I finally figured out that we weren't who we said we were, well, that would probably piss most people off. I was angry because I felt abandoned to raise two kids pretty much on my own while he went off in search of himself. I was angry because I believed him when we made our vows. I was angry because I felt betrayed. He's angry because—well I'm not really sure why he's angry, but he is, and I'm sure he feels as justified as I do.

Of course in retrospect, this is also why I have trouble finding love for myself. I now know I didn't believe being loved was possible for me. Hidden between the lines in my fairy tale book of love was the story of hurt and betrayal, so of course that's what I got. But the truth is, even though I understand my own part in our love tragedy, I still can't find any love for him anywhere in my being. Sometimes I hate him with the white-hot intensity of a thousand suns (fyi, that is my saying; I say it a lot, especially when I really, really hate something; I mean, if you gotta hate something it should be that hot, no-match-for-fires, here-I-go-all-the-way hate)—my anger runs that deep, mostly because I feel I have been willing to uncover the ugly parts of me in our marriage, while he hasn't. He still blames me and that makes me mad. Clearly there's more work to do on that. But the more I tried to act the part of spiritual master and show him love, even as I felt he showed me none, and asked myself that wonderfully spiritual question "What would love do here," the more I wanted to shove a dozen roses, thorns and all, down his throat. I wasn't being authentic. How could I do what "love" wanted if I didn't feel any? The more I tried, the more I didn't love him and the more I didn't love myself. I hated myself for lying to myself, for lying to appease my friends who were abuzz with the notion of peace and forgiveness for him, because that's what spiritual people do, right? They forgive you, even when you're an asshole. I wasn't there yet, and I was lying to myself in order to achieve some artificial peace prize. A spiritual Girl Scout badge with a big heart on it that said, "I love everyone, even if I think they are jerks!"

Once I let go of this notion that I have to love everyone unconditionally, I actually felt peaceful. I felt calm, and I felt compassion for myself. I felt lighter, and here's the really odd thing: when I looked in the mirror I started to like myself a whole lot better. Once I was free to just be honest about how I felt, not only about my ex-husband but about other people in my life, other situations in my life, I felt a freedom to be honest about everything and to see that I could also be compassionate about it. I finally understood what it meant to love myself.

I am short. For years I hated being short. I hated my short stubby little legs, so instead of trying to pretend I loved my legs unconditionally, I found compassion for them. They're just legs, and it's not their fault they're short, and there's not a whole heck of a lot they can do about it. So I forgave them; I accepted them. My ex-husband is a human, full of flaws like me. While I do not have to love him, I cannot change him, so I accept that he is who he is, and I accept that to him, I am who I am. It often isn't pretty, warm, and fuzzy—and believe me, there haven't been roses for a long time. But in being honest about it, I found peace, and in peace, I guess there is love.

When I tell my kids they have to love themselves and they give me that look, I often walk away feeling like I just sold out and took the easy route, once again passing on an unrealistic expectation and leaving them to hopefully figure it out one day. I have written a lot about my issues with my body and my sadness about the fact that my daughter carries the same belief. I have wondered about what I could possibly do to try to shift that belief. As I have come to learn, when you sit with a question and wait for an answer, you'll often find it comes when you least expect it. My daughter is quite the fashionista. I swear this girl was born with Gucci genes, and I love it when she helps me get dressed to go out. One night, as I tried on about ten pairs of jeans and tossed them into a pile on the floor, my daughter asked me why I didn't just pick one. I looked at her and shared that the truth was, I was frustrated with my body. I wanted longer legs and a tighter stomach, and I wanted to look like all the pretty girls I saw on the covers of magazines. She said to me in that sage voice of hers, "I know what you mean. It's hard because I don't look like that either." I took her hand and walked her over to the mirror. I said, "It's okay to not like things about your body. If you can, you work to change them by eating healthy and exercising, but don't do it because you want to impress other people. I mean, look at me. I've got chubby legs, and my stomach has stretch marks, and at first glance it's easier to say ugh! But then I remember how I got those stretch marks—giving birth to two wonderful kids—and I look at those legs and remember that they've carried me on many journeys throughout my life."

We looked at our bodies and played a game of finding the parts we loved, and then we looked online at the starlets we were trying to emulate and found pictures where they weren't all dolled up for the cameras. We decided Miley Cyrus could put on a few pounds and Charlize Theron probably hated her butt too. We realized we have allowed the expectations of others to dictate what we think we should look like, based on unrealistic criteria. There is nothing wrong with wanting to look beautiful, to feel good in your own skin and the Lucky Brand jeans you're covering it up with. There is always a way to find that beauty, but it's not by copying someone else; it's by working with what you have. My son said he loved my squishy tummy because it was nice to lay his head on, and my daughter said I had beautiful eyes and a great smile. We found our beautiful parts and accepted the parts that don't fit the standards society has set. That's when you love yourself, zits and all.

There is a prayer we've all heard: "Lord, grant me the serenity to accept the things I cannot change, the courage to change the things I can, and the wisdom to know the difference."

So, um, "love unconditionally?" Perhaps one day when I'm "enlightened" I'll do that, but for now I'll just "love authentically." What's that? It starts with acceptance, which to me doesn't mean resignation or defeat, it means allowing yourself to be honest about how you feel while accepting the things you cannot change and changing the things you can. It means showing compassion while telling someone something they don't want to hear, but saying it anyway, which is really showing unconditional love. But most important it's about giving yourself the permission to just be who you are and the willingness to change, when you're ready, and if you want to.

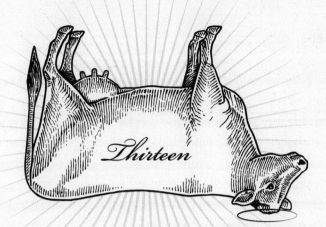

Thoughts on Forgiveness and Anger

Forgiveness, without a doubt, is one of the most complex and harrowing things we humans can endeavor to do as we navigate our lives. It requires a great turning and bending of our egos and of our judgment and a deep understanding of our beliefs about who we are.

Forgiveness is an act that requires recommitment, because we do not just forgive once—we often have to forgive the same thing every day over the course of days, weeks, months, and even years before it sticks. We have to choose forgiveness.

Forgiveness encompasses a space that is embedded in the core of what we consider the true self. It is where our trust and our identity story reside, and it is the place from which we pull out the gift of these vulnerable bits of ourselves and hand them over into another's hands with the return promise that those pieces will be treated with care. When forgiveness is required, it means that some part of our truest self has been bruised or broken or even irreversibly rewritten.

So, yeah, harrowing and complex.

Forgiveness has a great PR team. Check it out, we are told different cultural mores—forgiveness is what good people do; we must forgive; you can't heal if you don't forgive; forgiveness is needed to be able to move on; forgiveness is holy, enlightened, and good. It's all about forgiving. Forgive and you'll feel better, you'll find peace, you'll be enlightened. You MUST forgive. Do IT. Do it NOW, Earthling. Forgive, forgive, forgive. Buy my knives, my abs-defining belt, my life-fixing mojo.

But what if forgiving doesn't really do any of that?

When you really look at forgiveness, there is a basic premise that seems to be assumptive: the idea that forgiveness is great, that it is always right, and that you always must do it to move forward. And while at a higher level of consciousness that might be true, I will say that sometimes it feels like forgiving just for the sake of feeling better isn't really all that enlightened.

I would like to offer a different take: forgiveness as an option, not a necessity.

When I really look at the blanket-esque approach to forgiveness, it starts to seem like it's this thing we're supposed to swallow because they say it's good for us, sort of like a magic forgiveness pill—if you just swallow it, the pain will melt away. But, if forgiveness is a pill, wouldn't it be kind of important to talk about the potentially hazardous reactions we might have when we swallow it? I mean, you've seen those television commercials for the latest and greatest drugs, and they always seem to have a long list of side effects far more dangerous or disconcerting than the condition they're supposed to be solving (seriously, if I'm being forced to choose between patchy skin and the possibility of experiencing a debilitating stroke or death, well, I know what my choice is going to be). It just seems like blanket forgiveness needs a disclaimer too, because if you haven't really actually forgiven, it's just another lie to appease someone who quite frankly doesn't deserve to be appeased. And more important, it's a lie told to you by you. And we've already told ourselves enough of those.

There is also this other underlying thing that has to do with how people seem to very often *hear* forgiveness as "that's okay." An example of what I mean: one of my kids hits the other. I say, "Apologize right now, and ask to be forgiven." My contrite child says, "I'm sorry." And my other child says, "That's okay." And comforts the person who did the hitting. This is how forgiveness, in a very real way, acts for many people. Stop for a moment, and think about how dangerous that is. In essence, when we forgive, there's a good chance that the person who hurt us is hearing us say that whatever they did to hurt us is actually acceptable behavior, but that's not always okay.

This means that forgiveness needs to really be treated with care, with thought, and with the basic understanding that forgiveness is multidimensional. Along with the variation on how it's heard, just take into consideration the idea that sometimes you are supposed to forgive something or someone else, but sometimes you are really supposed to forgive yourself. You can also forgive the person someone was, because who they currently are isn't the person who hurt you. You might also be expected to forgive an action, because a person is not what they do. Or so I've been told, which seems very not right. If I choose to kick someone in the ribs just because I can, doesn't my choice to do that to someone make me a dick? The action is just the result of the choice; the choice is purely coming from a person. Just saying.

To add to that, in any situation that needs forgiveness, we can be the person who is doing the forgiving or the person who needs forgiveness. Or we can be both. This is a bummer all the way around, because it means that you have been hurt or you're the asshole who hurt someone or you both did a lot of hurting back and forth at each other. It's a suck-suck scenario.

We also have a plethora of ways in which we try to cope with whatever our role is when forgiveness becomes necessary in a relationship. Especially if your role is that of the "asshole." As an example, one of the most "Hey, let me add some irony-salt to your wound," schmuck-ish ways to cope is to be one of the people who suggests that the person who has been harmed should take the forgiveness pill so "everyone can move forward." This puts the hurt person in the position of either forgiving you or being responsible for holding everyone back. Real nice (God, we can be such assholes).

We do this because guilt sucks and because if you have hurt someone and need forgiveness, it means you have been an asshole. No one wants to be, or see themselves, as an asshole, even (or maybe especially) if it's a one-off or super infrequent thing. It's a way to feel better without ever having to deal with the fact that we have actually hurt someone, someone we probably know and care about. It also means that we probably won't have to do the hard work that is necessary to earn true forgiveness. Because forgiveness is not something I think should be asked for. Instead, it should be earned through actions. If you made a choice to take an action that hurt someone, you should make a choice to take an action to be forgiven. At least that's the way I see it. It's not on them, it's on you (the asshole in this scenario).

The role of asshole is to be avoided; I state the obvious because I am a master, having practiced the art of assholery many times in my life. There are ways to do this and I have figured them out through rigorous study and something called common sense. Thankfully, these ways are pretty freaking basic. Here they are: Be kind. Think before you speak or act. Treat others as you want to be treated. And that should get 'er done and help with the whole avoiding-being-a-schmuck thing. Lesson learned until I screw it up again. We are human after all—we fail. But I am trying to not fail so obviously in the future.

But this forgiveness thing is not even half covered. Not even a quarter covered.

Now let's talk about the role that is the one that messes with us in all of the places we are vulnerable and fucks with our trust. This is the role of *I have been hurt in a way that was not necessary, not allowed, not tenable, not okay, not permissible.* And I want to discuss what it means to take the path of righteous delayed forgiveness or outright righteous nonforgiveness. I use righteous for both of these paths because to be righteous means that your action is justifiable and in response to an injustice done to you. It is saying that what happened was not morally ambiguous to you. It was bad, to whatever degree it caused you hurt.

The other day my daughter came home very upset about something someone had said to her. I went into how she should ignore it, forget about it, understand the other person's pain . . . blah . . . blah . . . blah . . . all the colloquialisms I could muster out of my How to Be Spiritual and Enlightened Handbook, and then she looked at me and said, "You know what, Mom, it really hurt my feelings, can't I just be hurt for a minute?"

And it made me stop dead in my tracks as I realized in an ah-ha-and-wow way that she was spot on. She spoke up in that moment for her right to take the path of righteously delayed forgiveness and to acknowledge that she had a right to say that someone treated her in a way that was not allowed. It was her right to say that and make an internal judgment that what had been done to her was bad and that she was not the cause and that she was not obligated to take action on what another person had chosen to do. In other words, she was not obligated to forgive. The impetus to take action was not on her but rather on the perpetrator. My kid—she is a constant ah-ha-and-wow machine of livable enlightenment.

The truth is, when people do things to hurt you, you feel it—physically and emotionally. To ignore it, stuff it away, and pretend to be some shining light of spiritual forgiveness when all you really want to do is feel the hurt is actually hurting you more.

All of this was brought home to me a few days later when I came face to face with two people who have hurt me badly. For a long time I had been trying to swallow the forgiveness pill and each time it came back up covered in bile.

Why, after nine and half years of marriage, did I finally ask for a divorce? Because my husband was having an affair. It was not his first, but this time it was with someone who was supposedly my friend. Now, my marriage wasn't perfect, I wasn't perfect, our divorce was messy, and I am guilty of shooting off a rage-filled email or two (maybe three or four . . . okay, maybe more than that), but this revelation, a betrayal of our vows, truly hurt me in ways he probably doesn't even understand.

As I have revealed throughout this book, I have my own dark secrets about my beliefs, my insecurities, my fears, but this one act of betrayal reached into my core, my foundation, and ripped it apart. At the time, we were making a huge change in our lives. We were moving from our home in Washington State to California, and I didn't really have work, so in terms of timing, it sucked. Not only was my heart broken, but I felt as if I had been abandoned at a time when I didn't have my own means of income to raise two young children on my own. On top of that, it caused a great deal of pain for my children, so I had to watch and experience their pain as well.

Now in retrospect, one could argue this was the best thing ever to happen to both of us. And maybe it was, but at the time, being force-fed the forgiveness pill, especially by the people who had caused me such hurt, was not on my agenda.

During this time I received countless emails from my husband and his now wife/my ex-friend telling me how horrible I was, how I should just get over it and move on. Of course they wanted me to move on; they had yet to take any responsibility for their actions, and if I just up and forgave them, they would never have to speak any words to acknowledge that their actions had caused me great pain, even though they knew I felt that pain. There was a lack of basic empathy and compassion in their expectation that the onus was all on me to be the enlightened one and forgive them. Was this so that they could carry on hurting me, rid themselves of guilt, claim their schmuck cards, or what? Um—I can move on—but I will not forgive you. You won't get off the hook this time. I was justifiably hurt and justifiably mad. Righteous, if you will, in my choice to not forgive them.

Now, I know that it takes two (or in this case three) to tango, and I have offered an apology for my part in things to the person I caused hurt to, my ex-husband. The other, the ex-friend, was simply being a bully, attempting to hide her own shame over her behavior, her simple lack of understanding of the "chick code," and to her I offered no apology.

I offered my apology in person, in writing. I even wrote a blog about it*—I believe in covering my bases. And therein lies one of the many rubs in terms of this forgiveness thing. Because with each apology I gave for whatever hurts I had caused in our marriage and with each slap in the face I received back, forgiving became harder and harder. Because I realized I couldn't forgive in this case until the other parties did their part, but the only thing they were doing was demanding that I forgive and get over it.

I know that at some point it's about my own peace—but right then, standing in front of them in the courtroom, my peace was being true to how I felt. My own peace was learning to stand up for myself and say, "You know what, what you did is not okay. And guess what—you can't do that to me anymore." You can call me bitter, but it's not really bitterness that you're seeing. Instead, it's a refusal to accept that anyone is allowed to treat me in a way that hurts me.

Being able to say, "That is wrong, and I should be angry about it no matter how much time has passed," is, in terms of the forgiveness we are taught, considered a B.A.D (bad attitude, dammit). But maybe if we discussed it in another way, we could see that it might be time to revise our general forgiveness approach as a culture. For example, if someone punched your friend in the face, would you tell your friend that she shouldn't be angry at that person? Punching other people can be a crime, and we even arrest people for doing it, but we still expect each other to let any anger go, to forgive the act and the person, and to understand the why, as if the why somehow justifies the punch. Society is allowed to hold on to the wrongness of punching via laws, but the individual is still supposed to stop being angry. Why? Is the action somehow less bad because of the passing of time and distance and the fact that there might have been some underlying reason for the punch? It seems to me that a person should be able to say, "I was punched, and I am angry about that." Period. No time limit. When they think about it, they get to pull out the righteous anger card. Righteous. That word covers a lot of ground on this topic.

I think it is because we have made "angry" bad, culturally speaking. This could just be me, but I don't think so. Here's a cow to tip: anger can be good. It can be appropriate. It can be safe. It can protect in a good way. It can give impetus.

It's all about the context and how we channel our anger. This is what I think makes anger good or bad. For example, say someone kicked me in my ribs, and I am angry that I was treated that way. I can either go out and start beating up anyone who kicks (bad), or I can start an anti-kicking society that creates programs to help stop the cycle of kicking (good). Check me out, I'm complex! Humanity for the win!

And just because something that was done to us makes us angry, and the person who did it to us makes us angry, it doesn't follow that the anger automatically consumes us and stops us from moving forward. This would mean we are one-dimensional in our emotions, which we know is not the case. I can feel love and anger all at the same time. I can feel good about being angry while I am feeling angry and still understand that my anger is something that I need to be careful with.

I can be angry that people get kicked in the ribs and still go about my daily life. We *should* be angry about injustice. And that, in the end, is really what we are talking about here. When a wrong is done to us that causes emotion or physical pain, we have had, in a very basic way, an injustice done to us. And when put that way, the blanket-esque, forgiveness pill approach seems like silly sauce.

When I came face to face with my ex and his new wife, standing defiantly in court that day, I called them out. I let them know I wasn't going to let them off the hook. It wasn't pretty, and I wasn't the epitome of grace. I was exactly as I felt—hurt and betrayed and angry, and you know what? I'm freaking righteously okay with that. What they did to me was unfair and wrong. I was done pretending to be forgiveness-girl. And I spoke the truth, and this truth wasn't pretty or graceful. Forgiveness-girl exited stage right and real-time, angry Betsy entered stage left. It felt good. And not in an unhealthy way, but in a boundary-building, self-respect-having way.

The trick here is that I don't carry the hurt and anger around with me all day and let it fester. I aim it where it needs to be aimed and only when needed. That day in court, I did something that surprised even them. Instead of pretending, instead of taking the "high road," I took the real road. I declined the pill. I let it out, and I felt much better after.

Twenty-one years ago I had a friend. Not just any friend, a great friend, a best friend—the kind of friend you hope to have all your life, one that when you're eighty, you'll laugh at all the crazy things you did together. My friend Eric and I worked together at *Playboy*, we traveled the world together on many an adventure, and he was the person who helped me start my first production company. Eric is the shoulder I cried on when my boyfriend broke up with me, and I was the friend who helped him out of a pinch or two with a girl he should never have hung out with in the first place. If ever there was someone I could trust, it was Eric.

And I burned him. I burned him over money and success and career. With one selfish choice, I ruined something that could never be built again. Or so I thought. Thirteen years would go by before Eric and I spoke again. Thirteen years filled with guilt and shame over my behavior and grief over the loss of his friendship. And all because of a stupid choice I had made when I was twenty-three. That's a lot of shame and guilt. Then, one day out of the blue, my phone rang and up popped his name. Against all odds his number had been kept safe in my computerized contacts over the years—technology is awesome and, well, somewhat freaky.

I stopped dead in my tracks as I stared at his name. *Bleep* had come out, and I was "successful" again. Could he be calling because he was finally going to release those topless photos we took while on a shoot in Jamaica? Was he finally going to exact his revenge upon me for the hurt and pain I had caused him all those years ago? Unsure of what to expect, I let it go to voice-mail, but the moment it dinged on my phone, I listened intently to the message. He sounded congenial, but I worried that it could be a ruse. Then I searched my heart and remembered Eric. Kind, honest, and thoughtful Eric. Soft-hearted Eric.

So I called him back, jittery in my stomach but willfully open to what might come. If he did release those photos, I probably deserved it. I dialed, he answered, and I was gifted with my friend, the Eric who is kind and honest, and in that moment he taught me about forgiveness, and he taught me how to apologize.

He told me that he had seen *Bleep* and that he just missed me. He missed our friendship more than he remembered what I had done or what he might have done. Neither one of us asked for forgiveness; it was implied, it was instantly given, it was felt in the depths of who we had become thirteen years later, grown up, a little wiser and better able to value friendship over money or work. He showed me courage, because in reality, he had no idea how I would respond to him. All he had was a hunch and the courage to pick up the phone. Not to ask for anything, not to offer me a pill or to persuade me to offer him one, just to be friends again.

Perhaps one day my ex-husband, his wife, and I will have one of those moments. But not that day in the courtroom, because I just wasn't ready. And that is the key to forgiveness. It isn't about them, it's about you. And it's not about forgiveness either—it's about acceptance. There is a big difference between forgiveness and acceptance. I accept fully what happened in my marriage, I accept my part in our divorce, but I don't forgive the way in which it ended.

Nobody actually needs to "forgive." That is a cow, a big fat shit-colored one. What you need to do is find peace with your-self and acceptance of the act that occurred that caused you hurt. I am happily living my life and, except when I am forced to deal with them, it's great, and that's real right now. I have accepted them for who they are and what they are capable of, which perhaps will change. I'm no longer worried about when and if I'll forgive. I am going to protect myself, stand up for myself, and be real, and it's too bad if they don't like it. And I am okay if it isn't "enlightened." It's real, it's honest, and I have no need to appease anyone for their sake.

So I told my daughter that she should feel the way she feels, allow her experience to be had, and forgive only if she feels it's right within her and then she can let it go. Because that is what is important. Forgive when it feels right, not just because it's the pill you're expected to take to mask the symptoms of pain that make other people feel uncomfortable.

But with the right to *not* forgive comes the wisdom of letting go. You can let go of the hurt. You don't have to carry it around like a badge on your Girl Scout sash, all gold and glittery and reading, *I was betrayed!* Hanging onto the hurt is what makes you bitter. When you get stuck in the anger in a not-good way, when you play the victim for too long, you give your power away to your hurt, and you can become forever lost in its shadow.

Letting go of the pain takes time and it takes work: work on yourself to understand the part you may have played in that betrayal, if any; work to find a way to protect yourself from having that hurt occur again; and work to understand how to move away from the hurt. The hurt does not define you. It happened and it hurt. Experience it, put it on your wisdom-shelf for future reference if necessary, and live your life. In the case of my ex-husband, I did eventually forgive him—I took the path of delayed forgiveness. But it wasn't easy, and it wasn't on his or anyone else's timeline. It was on my own.

That path of delayed forgiveness can become the path of nonforgiveness. And sometimes going straight to righteous nonforgiveness is the truest response to a hurt caused by an untenable injustice. Because while the hurt my daughter and I felt in our relationships was painful and harmful to each of us in its own way, there are some hurts that step past what our brains can comprehend or reason into understanding. These are the hurts that bring us to our knees, curl us up, and make us want to disappear to escape the hurt. These are the hurts that cause such cracks in our trust and our selfhood that no amount of restoration will smooth them over.

Should we ask anyone to forgive the person who molested or raped them? Who beat or abused them? There is an aspect of forgiveness that requires acceptance, and some things are just not acceptable.

There is a statistic that is frightening: one in four women has been the victim of rape or molestation in her life. I'll say that again. One out of every four women on this planet has been raped or molested. I am that one in four.

In the moment when it first occurred, every ounce of trust and faith I had in men evaporated instantly. Clearly this is where the root of my feelings of unworthiness, my never feeling safe, and my need to be protected came from. It was a kick, a punch, a brutal assault on my childhood self. The cracks from this blow spidered out and touched everything and made me vulnerable to criticisms about my body, my intelligence, and my perceived value to myself. Sometimes the cracks filled my beliefs, making them fragile, and sometimes my beliefs filled the cracks, solidifying them. Much of my quest, my search to find all types of meaning to and in life, stems from this place, this red shirt of my past. Pain is often the impetus for spiritual questing, and I would be remiss to not speak to this early pain, this root of so many other hurts that have dominated the different stages of my life.

I share this piece of my reality rarely, and when I do, I am often asked if I forgive the man who did this to me. What I say in response is, Forgive? No. Accept? Yes. Because the truth is, and this is the hardest for many to understand, that I am who I am because of all of the moments of my life. They are my paintings, flawed and ugly, beautiful and grand.

Each moment of my life is inextricably my life. Accepted yes, forgiven sometimes, but angry still. How is that possible?

Because my anger isn't at him anymore. It was once, but now it's at us, me, you, the world. This is why I am writing this book. Because I'm angry that somehow humanity forgot the basics. Somehow we have lost our ability to love each other and respect each other, and our hurt manifests in how we hurt each other and then we become desperate for forgiveness because we feel shame. There is a part of me that would undo those moments of confusion and terror at the hands of a man trusted by me and my family, but the truth is I can't, and if I did, I wouldn't be me. But what I can do is try to help people understand how we work and how to find the true self that would never think of harming another. Because the way I see it, we must all work together. This is my way, although there are other ways as well. Maybe I'm naïve in that I believe that somehow love and understanding will help heal the world and somehow stop the cycle of abuse.

But this isn't just forgiveness. This is life. And though I may naïvely hope that somehow love and understanding will fix the world, I am still realistic. I fully believe that there are things in this world that are wrong, done by people who are just plain bad. People who are wrong on the DNA level. What do we do with that? How do we forgive something and someone who is just plain not right, who is wrong in all directions? Sometimes there are just bad people and nothing will fix them.

One in four—that is the statistic. So I am not the only one I know who has been molested. I have a friend who also experienced this in her childhood. We do not agree on some points of how to deal with forgiveness and acceptance in the scope of our pain caused by the betrayal and injustice of being abused. I am adding her story here because I think it is important to say that forgiveness or nonforgiveness is a choice, personal and profound, and as different as a thumbprint for each person.

My friend was molested as a young child, starting from the age of five and lasting until the age of nine. The abuse was severe—that is the only way I have ever heard her describe it. I know that she suffers from post-traumatic stress and that she still wakes up crying and covered in a cold sweat. My friend is complex, as people are, and she can be a shit. She is also hilarious and punny in the cheesiest of ways. Her trust is a distant thing, which is not surprising, so when she gives it, you know she has given you a true gift of herself. But as distant as her trust is, her empathy overflows. She is incredibly brave and amazingly kind. I love her profoundly.

We lost touch for a while and then reconnected in that way that can happen, and over a bottle of wine (or three) we caught up on each other's lives. She told me about something she had come to realize. She realized that she was angry over what had happened to her. She said it like it was a revelation. I think it was because of that whole "anger is bad" concept, and that she had not allowed herself to really go there, ever, about what had happened to her.

"I'm so incredibly angry, but not in a bad way," she said. "It's totally maintainable. It feels good and right." Which stuck with me.

I got it, this idea of being angry but not thinking of being angry as something that needed to be fixed or stopped. She is a happy person, living a happy life. Like me, she doesn't carry her abuse around with her. She doesn't even let her PTSD impact her life wholesale. She treats it like a chronic illness, something to be managed. She has compared it to a brain imbalance—she was injured in such a way that it messed with her chemical responses and the building of her neural pathways. Profound trauma can do that to you.

I recently called her and asked her about that anger and she said, "It's like my anger is screaming in a language that understands injustice." That was the best way she could describe it, she said, and she apologized for not being able to really encompass it for me and for making it sound cheesy. I told her what she had said was just fine.

She spoke about it in a very calm and accepting way—not of being molested, but of being angry. She went on to say that she felt okay with her anger, comfortable, because she felt it was a good and right anger. It didn't consume her; she knew it was something that a person should feel angry about in the same way we feel angry when someone is killed in a senseless shooting. That the act, the thing that was done to her was in every way wrong and bad and against everything we would consider to be right or good. Then she said, "Bad does not require my forgiveness, and I refuse to be passive in the face of it. I refuse to be anything but angry that such a thing happened to a child. I was that child. A horrible wrong was done to me. And I do not forgive the person who did that wrong to me. Because he is a bad man. Seriously, just plain bad. Why should society forgive that? Why should society 'let the anger go'? Why should I? It is part of who I am."

I have to say, I get this line of thought. Think about it. As a subject matter, molestation is pretty enraging—this violation happens to children; grown people do this to babies. Let's all be outraged here and not move on when the subject comes up. This is not something that deserves forgiveness, and we may be right to delay it or withhold it. We should remember it so that we are angry enough the next time it happens to do something serious about it. To point and say, "Stop that bad man—he's doing a great wrong." Maybe, if we weren't so quick to forgive, to forget, to jail, or to execute, we would make more progress in stopping the things that hurt people.

"Sometimes," my friend said, "forgiveness seems to anesthetize us to the point that we are unresponsive to what we should be absolutely in an uproar about." This is one of the side effects of the forgiveness pill when taken en masse by society. We really don't forgive child molesters. But we are "bad" if we judge and say we don't forgive, so we do on a deeply personal level when it happens to us.

It is weird that the general thought is that somehow our refusal to forgive and forget means we have not moved on. My anger, and I'll bet my friend's, keeps me diligent and more aware, not in a crazy kind of way but in a way that says, "Hey, pay attention here—something is not right." It is a way that takes action to correct a wrong, whereas if we were drugged with forgiveness, we might fall asleep at the wheel.

And that's just another bit of complexity to grapple with. Really, the complexity is endless. I mean, shit, I can even feel empathy for the sex offender who gets harassed when his neighbors discover he's on the sex-offenders registry. How weird and crazy is that bit of our human being-ness in action?

So there you have it: two different people, each with her own complex inner world of forgiveness and nonforgiveness. We are fully capable of understanding the other's choices and just as capable of not forcing our own decisions on the other. When and if she chooses to forgive is something she gets to decide. Ditto for myself.

Great wrongs do not require my forgiveness, nor do those who have done those wrongs. They simply require my understanding, if I am able, my acceptance of them, and my willingness to not let them define me.

Like a bad habit we should kick, we should really reconsider the knee-jerk impulse to take the forgiveness pill. Just like any drug, it's not right for everyone in every situation. So I say, let's give complexity a chance, and wisdom, and our ability to manage both in a way that answers our needs—in a way that makes us say, *Yes, this is good for me.*

Note

* If you feel like checking out the blog post, it can be found here http://intentblog.com/making-peace-with-our-past/. I won't say it's a grand ol' time, but it made me feel better, for a time at least.

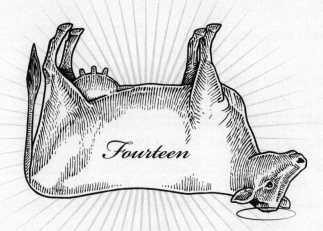

Fourteen

The Wrap

The hardest habit to break is the habit of being who you think you are.

—Vanda Mikoloski

L ife is a journey—that's the truest of truths—but how you travel is really up to you. Remember when you were five and your mom or dad, or adoptive parent, or uncle, or your crazy Aunt Matilda read you the Dr. Seuss books? Well, that was it, right there, in bold colors and print, with the Sneetches, the Whos, with Horton and Sam-I-Am, the Fox in the Socks, and the I ams, the Once-ler Sally, and Jo-Jo too. The Grinch figured it out eventually, and Dr. Smoot did as well. Those books pretty much told us how life was to be, if only we could grasp the concept of the metaphor at five. What an evil trick played on us, if you think about it. Sort of makes you wonder if there really is someone somewhere up in the heavens having a huge laugh at our expense. The wisdom of life, handed to us in full-color, simple text for the early reader, and all we really cared about was where the dogs were racing to.

In the words of Dr. Seuss, "You have brains in your head. You have feet in your shoes. You can steer yourself any direction you choose. You're on your own. And you know what you know. And YOU are the one who'll decide where to go . . ."[1]

Is it really that simple—can it be? The answer is yes, if we will only see. With eyes wide open and ears that can hear, the answers we seek are really quite near.

How many times have we passed the answer by, thinking, *It can't be that, it's too easy for me. I like to complicate things.* Most of us do.

One day about fourteen years ago, I had broken up with "the one" and was dating the next "one." He was yet another version of the same man I had dated for years—I must have just carried around the mask I wanted them to wear and when someone showed interest, I just slapped it on them and went for it. As I was leaving his house, doing my best walk of shame, I came across an old woman pushing her cart of belongings through the streets of the neighborhood. She looked at me and called me out: "The walk of shame . . . I've been there." I looked at her, stunned. Who was this person, bum even, to be telling me anything about life? She had obviously screwed hers up. Annoyed that she had actually picked up on my feelings of shame and unhappiness, as if she was a seer of things hidden deep, I grunted something and began to walk away. As I passed her, she said calmly and with more love than I think I had every truly experienced in my entire existence, "It doesn't have to be so hard, and it doesn't have to hurt so much. Why are you making it so hard on yourself?" I had no idea what she was talking about, because at that point in my life, I definitely did not have the eyes to see or the ears to hear, just a sad heart and no idea how to fix it. Hearing it from a homeless woman between Beverly and Melrose in Los Angeles wasn't really how I expected to gain the true meaning of life, yet since I had already blown off Dr. Seuss, I suppose beggars shouldn't be choosers.

Along came *Bleep*, and it seemed to give me the answers I was looking for. Little did I realize it provided the needed data but the integration was going to take a while. I lived in "I know it all" for a decade and then, after my existential crisis and the accompanying angsty hijinks, finally came to the place of "I don't know," and I'm okay with that. A few weeks ago, my son asked me if I knew who had been the first person here. How cool that he even pondered that question. I looked him straight in the eyes and said, "I have no idea. I've thought about it, I've read about it, and the truth is, I'm not sure. But if you've got a theory, I'd love to hear it." He contemplated quietly as my daughter chimed in, "I think we are made up of the stars—we are their wishes of who they'd like to be if they could be a person." Wow, pretty damn awesome if you ask me. Maybe she's paying more attention to Dr. Seuss than I did.

Once, before the beliefs set in and the emotions became rote, we believed in potential, we loved unconditionally, and we had no fears. We manifested without trying because our expectations were honest, and in truth we were the closest we probably would ever be to enlightened. And then we lived, and we forgot. We bought into the illusion, the matrix, and instead of *being* happy, we thought we needed to seek it, like that lost toy still hiding under the bed, behind the boxes we keep our dreams in because we no longer believe they'll come true. We're on the journey now, waiting to arrive, but where are we going and what's the rush? We're so busy trying to *do* what we should *be*, we don't take time anymore to really imagine or create what we could be. Essentially, we do create, just not what our souls desire. Instead we create from our box of broken crayons and torn papers because we don't dare ask for anything new, because deep down inside, we don't think we deserve a clean canvas on which to paint.

But what if you had one? What would you paint, and why aren't you painting that already? Now that you see what's keeping you from painting your dream, you can do the work necessary to paint that picture.

In the beginning, as I gazed upon my new empty canvas, I was frightened; what if I just painted the same thing, only slightly different? I looked around the room at all the shreds of my past, and I realized that there was one important thing I must do before I put pen to paper. I gathered up all my pieces, torn and thrown about in anger, judgment, and fear, in a rage of disappointment, and I took each piece, smoothed out its crinkles, wiped away the tears left on the page, and lovingly held it for a moment. I remembered each moment with gratitude. I knew that each one of those failures, hurts, betrayals, mistakes, and misdeeds given and received was a gift because with each one I grew and expanded my understanding of who I am and who I choose to be. Without them, I wouldn't be here, right here in this moment of freedom. Freedom from the dogmas of shoulds. Free to forgive, or not, free to feel how I feel, and free to paint the picture I want.

Often it is said that the New Age movement is all about "me," and to some extent that is true. Me is all we have, really. We're stuck with us. When the party is over and everyone goes home, we're left with ourselves. I believe that until I have cleaned up my own house, I cannot truly be of service to anyone else's. And if some think that's selfish or unspiritual, so be it. Just like the idea of stripping away the ego, this concept that we should be in service to others has gotten way out of hand.

Of course, giving of yourself to others is important. It creates community within you, and it feels good to feel connected to others, but once again, it comes back to you. There is no one who can tell you how to live a spiritual life but you. This idea that we should all forgive and forget is a menace to humanity. It is one of the greatest causes of unhappiness you'll encounter, because you are refusing to allow yourself to be the true authentic experience, and in forbidding yourself to be real, you are locking yourself into a prison of your own creation. "Better out than in," as Shrek would say.[2] The trick is to not get stuck in the muck of any one emotion or feeling. The trick is to be honest and do the work, and the work starts with you being honest with yourself.

Ultimately, life isn't about becoming enlightened or seeking happiness. The great Declaration of Independence got it wrong in my book. Happiness isn't a pursuit; it's a state of being already existing within us. Happiness isn't the prize.

How does one "just be happy"? That is the hardest and simplest answer of all. We choose it. We got into the habit of choosing unhappiness because we forgot we were in charge, and we confused the idea of happiness with pleasure. Happiness isn't about smiling all the time, loving all the time, or getting everything you want. It's about living and experiencing everything this life has to offer you, truly and authentically.

Okay, so I've had some fun. I've been silly, overly dramatic, probably made some outlandish generalizations and possibly some farcical analogies. But I bet if you take a moment, you'll see that we all do that, more often than we think. We put a lot of pressure on ourselves, and we create a lot of stress in our lives simply in our heads and then spend our day acting out the scenarios as if they are real, often making them real just so we can live them out. Shakespeare described the human condition best in *Macbeth*, Act V, Scene V: "Life's but a walking shadow, a poor player that struts and frets his hour upon the stage . . ." (dramatic!). But seriously, we are dramatic creatures, and it's time to have a good laugh at our expense. I did. I wanted to laugh at myself and the absurd things we put ourselves through in order to find that elusive happy place. Because ultimately, that is what we're all looking for. Call it enlightenment or call it living your bliss, free from those pesky attachments to people, places, things, times, and events in our lives that didn't live up to the barometer set by the spiritual, cool people.

But you know what, I already am at the pinnacle of being—the grand stage of enlightenment—because I am *being*. I know,

I know . . . that sounds so woo-woo and nebulous after I just wrote thirteen essays on why woo-woo and nebulous suck cow's balls. But that is because it is woo-woo and nebulous. Which is awkward if you are all like, "I can define every aspect of my existence without words like woo-woo." For me, the trick is loving the nebulous, loving the in-between, living in the moments that are what they are: struggle (suffering), joy and bliss, happy, sad, and everything in between.

I stopped striving to be something I couldn't be, and in doing that found happiness, all the aspects of happiness, all the layers of happiness, all the strings attached to the theories of being happy. They aren't theories anymore; they are possibilities, and I am free to grab on to any one I choose at any moment and make it real. I let go of being the material Betsy (and I don't mean that in the "I like to buy shoes" kind of material, because I do, and I'm not going to change that). In the materialistic science kind of way, I let go of the notion that everything is as it is—solid, static, black and white, no room for change—and I found peace in the color spectrum.

I gave myself permission to fuck it up, to forgive myself for fucking it up, and accept that I am going to continue to fuck it up. This isn't a permission slip to go out and be an asshole and then repent on Sunday. I must operate from a place of integrity, if not for the other beings in the world then for myself, because I have to be able to live with myself. I accidently create enough cow shit that I need to clean up, so there's no need to create any on purpose. People know what's in your heart—it shines outwardly, and you especially know what's hidden in the dark crevices of your spirit, your soul, so don't put anything down there you don't want to come back up as bile later on. That's just gross.

So often in my life and in the lives of those who have opened up to me, there is this desire to shove our true feelings way down deep. I've written in this book about my real feelings about my divorce, my childhood, and my parenting. I sort of feel all splayed out as if everyone reading this is examining the contents of my guts and it ain't pretty. Frightening thought, actually, but freeing too, because I am finally able to just be me, all covered in cow shit, laughing my ass off at the sight of me.

I I I

Now that you've had a chance to laugh and cry with me, do it for yourself. Live, feel, experience life, this reality, this dimension, because in my humble, not very spiritual but spiritual perspective, that is why I am here. I have answered the ultimate question for myself. I am here to live.

The only spiritual path that is right for you is the one you're on and the one you choose to take. Let go of the "right way." Let go of knowing and just live it with all you've got.

The greatest piece of wisdom I ever got was from a bumper sticker (hey, don't judge—it's freaking profound. I want no pointing and laughing about "bumper sticker philosophy." Profound, I tell you!). It said, "The truth shall set you free, but first it will make you miserable." I've learned to enjoy being miserable. I've finally figured out that being miserable often leads to great awakenings, great understandings, and some really good laughs later on. I've learned to find a foundation of being happy because the truth is, why not? That old saying "This too shall pass" is actually true. Even in the darkest of hours, I look around me and I see in the smallest of things something magical, something amazing. It's work in the beginning, but now it's not so hard for me. It's a sacred cow I'll keep. Even when it sucks.

Every day as I hang in that space between asleep and awake, before I put my feet on the floor and collapse my reality into being, I remind myself that today will be filled with challenges, unexpected moments of joy and sadness, and everything in between. I am so grateful for the opportunity to experience this. How cool it is to live! Then, that night, as I lay my head down to sleep, I smile and say, Wow, I made it. How cool was that? And I close my eyes and dream up the next adventure.

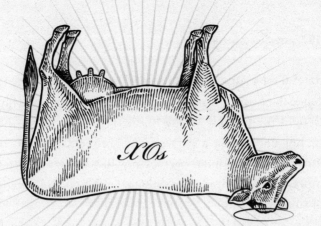

My life has been filled with so many amazing people. Even if I didn't think they were so amazing when they were in my life. If I could thank each and every person I've ever encountered in this life, I would, because each of you has had an impact on me in some way. Most important, you brought me here, to this now, and I wouldn't change a moment of it.

With that being said, there are some standouts. First and foremost I want to thank my children, Max and Elora: you are my greatest divine gift and my goddess of light. I am forever grateful for your coming into my life and allowing me to experience the tears of joy and utter frustration, both of which have brought me humbly to my knees. I want to thank their dad for not only being a part of what brought them to me, but also for being a huge part of my life. To say you made an impression is an understatement: thank you, you taught me a lot (in a good way).

I want to say how grateful I am to my mom, my rock—that woman gave me, and still gives me, more than she will ever know. I honor her, and every day she shows me what true love means. And my father, who left this reality a long time ago but is always with me. Thank you, Dad, for giving me the greatest gift, the ability to laugh even when it's hard.

I have such great women around me. My sister: thank you for always being there, ready, willing, and able to bake a cheesecake, make a prank call, or watch silly cat videos. You are awesome. And to my friends Cate, Gabby, Jennifer, and Janie, who have stayed on the phone and didn't hang up when I cried and railed against the world, who drank wine with me and laughed at the absurdity of our lives. For hours spent contemplating the universe and our hips, or which movie star we'd bed and which guru we'd bed, in no particular order, and what it means to love and to live—I have learned so much from you and am often in awe at how gracefully you maneuver through life and are patient when I break all the glass in your house.

To my dear friends and co-conspirators in creativity Ri Stewart and Renee Slade, thank you for opening my heart and my mind to what is possible, in life and in creating art. Thank you for showing me that even I am creative, for leading me back to my creative spirit, for listening as I rambled on, sometimes incoherently, about my vision, and for actually understanding what the hell I was saying and bringing it to life. And to my friend Jon Snow (the real one): winter is coming and I am so very grateful to have a friend like you to face the cold with.

Thank you to the teachers who spent time with me: Austin Vickers, Amit Goswami, Gini Gentry, Deidre Hade, and Dr. Joe Dispenza. You are an inspiration to me and your work has had a profound effect on me. Thank you for making all of this stuff make sense.

To my editors, Anna and Sarah—you two are saints. I don't even have words to describe my gratitude for the work you did with me in making my crazy make sense. And to everyone at Beyond Words, Atria, and Simon & Schuster, thank you for your love, support, and dedication to bringing words to our world so that we may learn, laugh, and cry while all snuggled up and reading.

And lastly to my dogs, Tara and Zach (I hope you have your tennis ball with ya, Zach, in whatever adventure you're on now), and to my cats, (Here and Gone) Spike, Jack Puppin, Max, Coco, Princess, Sophie, Obi, and Deedee. Even you are a great reflection: in picking up your poo and cleaning your litter box I have learned many a great life lesson. Who knew there was such wisdom in a hairball.

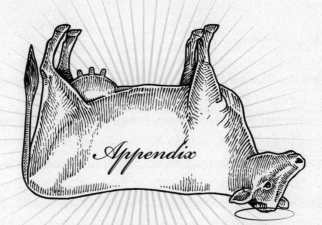

Appendix

(or Some Shit You Can Learn from Me)

There I am sitting at a dinner party having that wonderful existential conversation with friends over smoked salmon and wine. I'm wearing my I'm-so-wonderfully-spiritual mask, and so is everybody else (in immediate retrospect, it's kind of like a club, like the Elks Club people when they wear their nifty hats, except our club is a spirituality one and our hats are metaphoric masks on our faces). Someone has just finished a beautiful story about how they saved a dying bird from the jaws of their cat, giving it Reiki and sending blue light and love to heal it. The bird flits away, but not before stopping for a moment to look lovingly back at its savior.

As everyone oohs and ahs, I think to myself, *Okay, yeah I've saved a few birds in my life. But let's get real for a moment, Betsy* (yes, I am speaking about myself in the third person while writing in the first. I do this first because I can, and second because it's three something in the morning, and third—wheeeee). *Admit it. You've stomped giddily on a spider, lifting your foot to make sure it's squished into oblivion with a satisfied smirk on your face.*

I decide, with the same smirk I had when I smeared that spider into oblivion, that it's time to take off my enlightened-master costume and get real. It's fun to watch the horrified look on their faces when I reveal that underneath that mask I'm more like Darth Vader than Mother Teresa—I'm conflicted. I'm part human, part master, part little shit, and I'm okay with that.

I launch in on the story of my recent encounter with a dying possum, the possum who attacked my cat and left it for dead, the possum who has been snacking on my garden, the possum who creeps me out by lurking about at night while I sit in my yard. The ultimate asshole possum.

As it lay there bleeding on my concrete, I only thought about how I was going to need to get out bleach to clean up the mess the next day. I did not rush over to it, sending it healing whatever. I did not give it Reiki as it passed over to the next realm. I just waited for that sucker to die so I could get rid of it before my kids woke up.

Apparently, that was not very spiritual.

But you know what, it was real. And real is where I am at. As I have said, being spiritual isn't wearing bunny bliss slippers and rose-colored glasses. We are humans and humans are flawed and when you're hiding your flaws, when you're hiding your true feelings, you're not being—you're bullshitting. Bullshitting everyone around you and, more important, yourself. And if you truly want to be free from all the old paradigms, beliefs, and baggage and move forward in your life in a way that allows you to experience the happiness that's inside you, the happiness and peace you deserve, then it's time, as Dr. Phil would say, to get real (see, you can learn something from Dr. Phil. In between the fake tears and the slugfest there are some gems).

I like to play a game with myself, especially when my bullshit meter is screaming *Code 3! Code 3! You're lying to yourself!*

It's called "My Life Sucks," and it's designed as a way for me to get real about my feelings, about what I really believe underneath all the pithy quotes and "right" ways of being and doing.

There is a freedom in allowing yourself to be angry, to be disappointed, to be hurt, and to not judge yourself. To take some time in that space without analyzing the whys. I believe sometimes when we think we're "aware," we think we're supposed to pull some piece of spiritual wisdom out about a situation. We forget to allow ourselves a moment to just be what we are. It's tricky not to get stuck there—but I know I won't, I can trust myself to not do that—but the release of allowing myself to just be brings more clarity and acceptance than when I stuff it away. When I start to "work" on the feeling without giving myself time to experience it, to understand it.

So I invite you to play along—to give yourself the freedom to take the actual time to figure shit out. This invite is open ended, to include right now.

Letting it all hang out is, for me, the first step in healing, the breaking down of old patterns and the discovery of what my true desires are. Play the victim for a while, because deep down inside we are victims; we're just afraid to admit it. I have been a victim of my own creation. So I'm going to exercise my victim right now.

Note: I suggest, if you can, recording instead of writing out the games. When you're speaking, you can't judge yourself, edit yourself, or use an eraser. After you have recorded yourself playing the games, go back and transcribe what you said—and, oh yeah, don't edit it.

▮   ▮   ▮

I'm going to give you context to help with my example on how this works. I live in a full house with two kids, a grandmother, a dog, and, well, too many cats. So finding the time or the space to rant at the top of my lungs about my life sucking is not always easy.

I have found the best place to do this is in my car while driving, usually at night after my kids have gone to bed. With my mom home to watch them as they slumber, I jump in my car. I figure it's the most private space I have, right?

Which means that I, er, sometimes let loose while motoring along. Because it's private space (in my make-believe land, but whatever). So, this one time, when I was letting loose in my private space in a way that I suppose could be described as ranting. Okay, yes, I was ranting, ranting about an ex-boyfriend who was the cause of all my suffering. He was the reason I was insecure and unable to love fully and, on top of that, he had a really small penis! The fucking nerve.

As I screamed all of this at the top of my lungs, I got hung up on the word penis—it's a great word to say when you're mad. I repeated the words *small penis* over and over again, spitting and frothing (as one does when using the sm's and p's). What I had forgotten was that my window was down.

"Small penis, small penis, small penis!" That was me, all a-rant. Slow motion, my head turns. Smaalll peeenissss . . ." and there, next to me, was a really nice slice of manhood in a convertible. The detail about the convertible is only important because the top was down, which was like having his windows down to the power of four, plus a roof. So there we were, eye contact being made as just as I finished the extended "s" sound of penis.

Spoiler alert. I did not get his phone number. I did get an awesome visual representation of the words *gawked* and in *horror*. I pretty sure I gave a great imitation of "insane lady" as visualized through the lens of "Holy shit—she's going to cut off my penis!" Good times!

Disclaimer: when playing My Life Sucks, keep your hands in the ride, etc., and for the love of god, make sure you're alone and no one can hear you.

❚ ❚ ❚

Step 1: My life sucks: Say it loud and say it proud!
No really, it sucks. Don't hold back, really lay it all out on the line here. What really sucks about your life? Your job, your boyfriend, your car, your house, your nails, your hair, your body . . . really,

what sucks? Spend as long as you can listing everything that sucks about your life. But truly mean it and don't judge. If it popped into your head, you absolutely hate it, so say it, or write it down.

Examples: My shoes suck because I can never find my size. My clothes suck because I'm short. My car sucks. My boyfriend sucks. My furniture sucks. My garden sucks. My hair sucks.

I   I   I

Step 2: Why does it suck?

Does it suck because of your parents, your husband? Who or what made it suck? Now is not the time to go all Deepak on yourself and pretend you think you have some wisdom, because if you did, your life wouldn't suck. So be honest about why you think your life sucks.

Examples: My job sucks because the people in my office are Neanderthals and stupid and mean. My school sucks because no one likes my kind of music. My parents suck because they were broke and couldn't buy me anything.

Note: Don't judge! I know you . . . you're judging. Stop it! Scream it, yell it, sing it, sign it—whatever, but say it.

I   I   I

Step 3: Blame it on everyone and everything else.

Here's your chance. With no one listening, really let them have it. In this moment I give you permission to be the biggest victim you can be. Go back through as much of your life as you can remember and let those fuckers have it.

Examples: I'm short because of my damn parents. My body sucks because I'm short and I had kids and they ruined my body.

▮ ▮ ▮

Step 4: Acknowledge you're a failure. Yep, you failed.

Admit it—you have utterly failed at life. If you hadn't failed, your life wouldn't suck, right? So say it loud, and say it proud. I am a complete failure!

What have you failed at? Go back through your life and list every failure, no matter how small it might be. Don't let yourself off the hook, and don't hide behind some excuse. You failed—list it.

Examples: I failed because I didn't go to college, and that made it hard for me to get jobs, and I didn't go because my parents didn't save my money, and it's all their fault. I failed my kids because I got divorced and now they will be losers. I failed at marriage not once but twice, so now I know that I will never find love.

Note: Now is not the time to give yourself a pep talk. These thoughts are hidden deep within you. You know it, and I know it, and they aren't going anywhere unless you let them out, so do it!

Don't you feel better? Wasn't that fun! You did it. You blamed everyone, and you admitted you were a failure. All those little thought monsters that have been partying it up in your head for years are finally out on the table or the bed or in my case, the windshield of my car.

Okay, now what? You are probably feeling a little cranky and mad at the world. After all, you did just blame them for all your life's misery. Here's what.

I I I

Step 5: The release: Is anything I just said true?
Many of us will say no, it's not true. But if you don't believe it's true, why did you say it? There is a part of you that believes it is.

Why do you believe it's true? And do you still want to?

See, now you know what's really lurking in the deep recesses of your mind. And now, if you truly let it all hang out, you can pick up that sacred cow and examine it fully, from all angles, look at it all painted and sparkly. You can admire all the things you did to try to pretty it up, to make it spiritual, make it accepted, make it okay. And if you couldn't make it okay, and you just shoved it in the back where no one could see it and cobwebs formed and bugs moved in and it created a whole little world inside of you. Well, now it's out, front and center, and you can finally deal with it. Keep it if you want or let it go if you don't. That's the hard part: letting go of something that has become a part of you, ingrained in your skin.

I I I

Step 6: Awareness, acceptance, and forgiveness.
And this is the final step, one that you will repeat many times in your life. The first time I played this game, as I came to this step, I cried. Actually, I sobbed uncontrollably because I had never let myself feel any of this before and the relief, the release, was so profound that for days, even weeks after, I felt great. But the truth is, sometimes those fears, those beliefs try to sneak back onto my shelf. So I am aware, and I find the time to play My Life Sucks again, and I remind myself that I am human. My feet are planted on this earth, in this reality for a reason—to work this shit out. It's all going be okay: just do the work.

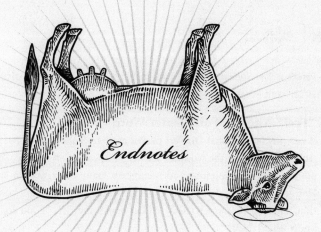

Endnotes

1. Red Shirts in Your Brain

1. *What the Bleep Do We Know!?* Directed by William Arntz, Betsy Chasse, and Mark Vicente. Theatrical release 2004. 20th Century Fox, 2005, DVD.

2. Enlightenment Says, Huh?

1. Immanuel Kant, *Foundations of the Metaphysics of Morals and What Is Enlightenment* (New York: Macmillan, 1990).

3. The Wacky Tale

1. John Gribbin, *In Search of Schrödinger's Cat: Quantum Physics and Reality* (New York: Bantam, 1984).

2. *The Quantum Activist.* Directed by Ri Stewart and Renee Slade. Theatrical release 2009. Intention Media, Inc., 2009, DVD.

6. Who Is the Universe?

1. Max Schlickenmeyer, "The Most Astounding Fact—Neil deGrasse Tyson," YouTube video. Audio from an interview with *Time* magazine. Posted March 2, 2012. http://www.youtube.com/watch?v=9D05ej8u-gU.

2. *People v. The State of Illusion*. Directed by Scott Cervine. Theatrical release 2012. Exalt Films, 2012, DVD.

7. "Feel," Another Four-Letter Word

1. I recently learned that Dr. Pert passed away in September of 2013. It was truly a sad day for the world of science and women in science. She was a pioneer and an inspiration—to me and to many other women and men. Her groundbreaking work will continue to inspire thoughtful contemplation, and I do hope you'll check out her books and CDs. If you do, you will know what I mean.

2. Candace B. Pert, *Molecules of Emotion: The Science Behind Mind-Body Medicine* (New York: Touchstone, 1997).

3. Joe Dispenza, *Breaking the Habit of Being Yourself: How to Lose Your Mind and Create a New One* (Carlsbad, CA: Hay House, 2012).

———, *Evolve Your Brain: The Science of Changing Your Mind* (Deerfield Beach, FL: Health Communications, 2007).

I have spent many an hour discussing these concepts with Dr. Joe Dispenza. Some are described in his books *Evolve Your Brain* and *Breaking The Habit of Being Yourself* and in *What the Bleep Do We Know?!*

8. Living in Bliss and Other Myths

1. *Finding Joe*. Directed by Patrick Solomon. Theatrical release 2011. Pat and Pat Productions, 2012, DVD.

11. Fear and Judgment, the Real Battle for Survival

1. *After Earth*. Directed by M. Night Shyamalan. Trailer. Theatrical release 2013.

14. The Wrap

1. Dr. Seuss, *Oh, the Places You'll Go!* (New York: Random House, 1990).

2. *Shrek*. Directed by Andrew Adamson and Vicky Jenson. Theatrical release 2001. Dreamworks Animation, 2001, DVD.

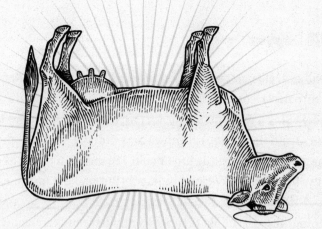

Tipped Cocktails

Okay. So you're probably wondering why there are cocktail recipes at the end of this book. I'm not suggesting that we all just get drunk and drown out our problems. However, there is something profoundly contemplative, thought provoking, and even a bit lighthearted in the ritualistic movements of mixing a cocktail. We must be present in our actions, lest we add too much of one ingredient and not enough of another—and life shouldn't be too sweet or too bitter! There is also the joyful feeling of expectation in our minds as we imagine what the cocktail will taste like, not to mention the satisfaction we get after mixing the perfect cocktail. If you think about it, mixing the perfect cocktail is a great metaphor for "mixing" your life. And besides, the truth is, if you're going to sit down and do the work necessary to create the life of your dreams, you might as well do it with a yummy cocktail in hand. (But make it just one, okay?)

I decided that since we already have a milky, creamy thing going with this book, then we should have milky, creamy drinks to go along with it. After all, aren't things just better when they're smooth and creamy? So, I called my mixologist, Gabrielle Sagona . . . (Wait. You don't have a mixologist? Well, just like having your own physicist, having your own mixologist is, like, so now.) I called her up, and we had a lovely time concocting yummy cocktails that fit our mood and provided the perfect balance to whatever we were working through.

Please note that each of these recipes serves one, and the average shot glass is equal to about 1 ounce (or 2 tablespoons).

The Banshee

Sometimes you're just angry at the world, but there is nothing like bananas and chocolate to bring you back to the serenity of love on a sidecar of the warm-and-fuzzies. The taste of banana and chocolate reminds me of being a kid and eating bananas while spreading peanut butter on each bite. Though there is no peanut butter in this drink, having chocolate is yet another simple little pleasure—one that makes being angry perfectly fine.

1 ounce banana liqueur
½ ounce white crème de cacao liqueur

1 ounce whole milk, or to taste
Grated dark chocolate, to serve (optional)

Combine the banana liqueur, white crème de cacao liqueur, and milk in a cocktail shaker with ice cubes. Shake purposefully. Strain into a chilled martini glass, using the dark chocolate as a garnish. Another fun option is to make a blended cocktail. Just add 3 to 4 ice cubes and blend away till it's smooth and frothy.

Velvet Hammer

Thor has his hammer, right? And let's be honest, Thor kicks ass with that hammer (and he's freakin' hot to boot!). While there are times when you may want to kick a little ass (or a *bunch* of ass) too, I've found that it's usually better to be firm while maintaining a delicate hand. So when you feel that retaliatory surge, pause, think, and remember: you packed a Velvet Hammer.

1 orange wedge (optional)
Cocoa powder (optional)
2 ounces Cointreau
2 ounces Tia Maria
2 ounces half & half

If desired, gain an extra bit of power by preparing your whiskey or rocks glass with a ring of chocolate grit: Rub the orange wedge along the rim of the glass, then dip the wet rim in cocoa powder before the juice dries.

Mix the Cointreau, Tia Maria, and half & half in your cocktail shaker with ice cubes and empty the contents into the glass with victorious flare!

The Tequila Rose

At times, life requires a little subtlety. You know the situation: you have to make your point, your mark, that first impression—claim your ground—and you really want to pack a wallop, but you don't want to scare anyone either, right? Just channel your inner Tequila Rose, who is sweet (tastes like cream-filled chocolate candy), but channel her judiciously, for she packs a punch you won't soon forget!

1 ounce Tequila Rose
½ ounce light rum
1 ounce chocolate liqueur
1 ounce half & half
1 fresh strawberry, to garnish (optional)

In your cocktail shaker, shake the Tequila Rose, light rum, chocolate liqueur, and half & half with ice cubes into a frothy fiesta! Strain into a chilled martini glass. Make a small cut in the strawberry to allow it to perch on the rim of the glass.

Dragon Punch

When you're playing with fire . . . well, you know what they say. So, when you're facing your fire-breathing dragons (i.e., your thought monsters), you better come prepared against the dragon's fire with something more than a shield. You need a secret weapon! Not to worry. Just mix up your secret potion of Dragon Punch and put that thought monster to bed for good.

To make simple syrup, you "simply" heat a solution of equal parts sugar and water, stirring until the sugar is dissolved. In the case of this drink, 1 tablespoon of each should give you enough to work with, and you can refrigerate whatever you don't use—for the next time a dragon comes your way!

1 ounce rum
½ ounce crème de cacao liqueur
1 ounce coconut milk, or to taste
Simple syrup (cooled), to taste
Skewer of fresh or canned pineapple chunks, to garnish
    (optional)

As with all these drinks, your personal tastes for balance should factor in to your Dragon Punch too. You may wish to adjust the levels of coconut and sugary flavor depending on how many thought monsters you're battling. Whatever the combination, shake up the rum, crème de cacao liqueur, coconut milk, and simple syrup with some ice cubes in a cocktail shaker, and pour that cool creation over more ice cubes in a rocks glass. Throw in the pineapple skewer (wood, bamboo, or plastic sword—all are equally lethal), and you'll be properly defended.